ALSO BY GERALD HAUSMAN

Meditations with Animals
Meditations with the Navajo
Turtle Island Alphabet
The Sun Horse

THE GIFT OF THE GILA MONSTER

Navajo Ceremonial Tales

INTRODUCED AND RETOLD BY
GERALD HAUSMAN

Foreword by Tony Hillerman

A TOUCHSTONE BOOK
Published by Simon & Schuster
New York   London   Toronto   Sydney   Tokyo   Singapore

TOUCHSTONE
Simon & Schuster Building
Rockefeller Center
1230 Avenue of the Americas
New York, New York 10020

Designed by Irving Perkins Associates, Inc.
Manufactured in the United States of America

1   3   5   7   9   10   8   6   4   2

Library of Congress Cataloging-in-Publication Data

Hausman, Gerald.
The gift of the gila monster: Navajo ceremonial tales/
introduced and retold by Gerald Hausman;
foreword by Tony Hillerman.
p.   cm.
"A Touchstone book."
Includes bibliographical references.
1. Navajo Indians—Religion and mythology.   2. Navajo Indians—
Rites and ceremonies.   I. Title.
E99.N3H373   1993
299'.72—dc20   92-32317
CIP

ISBN 0-671-76811-5

Art work on pages 31 and 101 is reproduced
by permission of Jay de Groat.

Acknowledgments

Although this book is based on stories heard by the author, corroboration was done at the Wheelwright Museum of the American Indian in Santa Fe, New Mexico. Curators Steve Rogers and Unis Kahn were helpful, and without their guidance and the use of fieldwork conducted by Mary C. Wheelwright, the stories would seem incomplete. In addition to the work of Mary C. Wheelwright, I have studied the original manuscripts of Father Berard Hailey. These two, probably more than any others, have contributed greatly to the preservation of Navajo ceremonial culture in written form. The unpublished writing of Mary C. Wheelwright gives an accurate record of Navajo ceremonials in English. Father Berard Hailey's work, however, appears in both English and Navajo. In addition, the works of Washington Matthews, Dr. Clyde Kluckhohn, Gladys Reichard, Franc Johnson Newcomb, Tony Hillerman, and Frank Waters have influenced this book. Hosteen Klah, Yohe Hatrali, Etsay Tso, Louis Big Man, Klahzhin Begay, Klahzhin Betselli, and others have given the Ways an authentic voice, the spoken rhythm of Navajo phrasing, as well as certain narratives.

Jay de Groat—friend, tribal historian, poet, ceremonial sharer, and painter—remains the heart and spirit of many of the stories. Ray Brown, who gave time to the project, believed the stories should be written down in order to preserve them, not only for his own children and grandchildren but for future generations. Loren Toledo shared his thoughts often enough over the last six years, and I am especially grateful to him for his friendship and his frequent confirmation of the work. Grateful acknowledgment is given to Mariah Fox for reproduction of sand-painting motifs. The careful editorial guidance given by Gary Luke, Megan Paris Rundlet, Isolde C. Sauer, Laura Ware, and Ricia Mainhardt has been invaluable. To all these people and especially, The People, my heartfelt thanks.

Contents

Foreword
Tony Hillerman

Since I grew up with Potawatomi and Seminole playmates and have lived most of my later life surrounded by Pueblo Indian cultures, I am often asked why I focus my mystery novels on the Navajos. The answer is too long to repeat here. It deals with the Navajo's remarkable sense of humor, with an unselfish value system rating care of family and clan members high and personal acquisitions low. It covers the high status the tribe has always given to women. But most of all, my fascination involves the Navajo religion and the complex system of poetry on which it is based. It involves what Gerald Hausman in this volume calls "the gift of the Gila Monster."

I am myself a believer in God, a would-be Christian, and specifically a Roman Catholic. As such I look into our origin story—the tales of the creation of Adam and Eve, of the murder of Abel, of the Tower of Babel, and the great body of mythology we call the Old Testament—and find in it a way of understanding humanity's relationship with our Creator. I look into the brief gospels that Christ left us and find my simple (if hard-to-follow) instructions on how to live. The traditional Navajo does the same in the metaphors of his Origin Story and in the teachings of Changing Woman, that greatest of all the Navajo spirits.

There are many similarities between the Jewish-Christian

story of our genesis and the poetry by which the Navajos explain how humanity came to be on earth. There are also many differences. As in our tale of man's expulsion from Eden, the fall of the Tower of Babel, the Great Flood, and the destruction of Sodom and Gomorrah, the Navajo Creation Story is one of stress between humanity and the supernatural, and of man's evil bearing the inevitable fruit of punishment. But the Navajo account of how humanity rose out of the dark "First World" is more abstract. It deals in an oblique way with evolution and how the gift of language separated man from the animals. Instead of offering the comfort of Christianity's personal God, who will love us if we let Him, it teaches a system of compulsory magic (which we might call applied psychology) by which man can maintain the harmony that makes life not only tolerable but beautiful.

I once watched the interview of an eminent astronomer by a reporter for British television. The astronomer was describing the "Big Bang" theory, which most agree was the origin of the universe as we know it.

The interviewer was not satisfied. "But what was there before this cosmic explosion? And what caused it?," she asked.

The astronomer seemed surprised. "Young woman," he said, "that is a nonquestion."

For those whose intellect takes them no further than the laws of physics, it is indeed a nonquestion. Seeking the answer takes us beyond mathematics and physics into metaphysics and therefore into a realm of thought with which the language of science cannot cope. Inspired men in the Euphrates Valley tried to explain the answer to the ultimate nonquestion. Lacking the words to express their vision, they gave us the metaphors of the Old Testament. Among the Athapascan-speaking people of northern Asia, inspired shamans did exactly the same. Something very similar happened in almost every culture of which I am aware. Humanity's hunger to understand why it exists, why it must die, and its purpose on this planet has always been satisfied by the genius of inspired poets, be they Semites, Modoc, Mayan, or Macedonian.

Since Navajo theology is more complex and abstract than Jewish-Christian metaphysics, Gerald Hausman can provide only a sample in his examination of the ceremonial stories of this remarkable people. But it is a revealing sample, astutely selected. It will give readers an understanding of how their people have earned the title "the Enduring Navajo" when engulfed by a dominant materialistic society hostile to their ways, and how they have maintained a culture that values human relationships above material possessions, abhors violence, rejects the concept of revenge, and teaches all who will listen that we should always go "with beauty all around us."

So it is that all these countless myth-dramas lead into still more myths and ceremonials. . . . All combining into one vast interlocked myth which is at once the complete story of The People and the whole story of man.

FRANK WATERS

Introduction

In 1885, after spending three years among the Navajo at
Fort Defiance, Arizona, Dr. Jonathan Letherman wrote in
the Smithsonian report of that year: "They have no knowledge of their origin or the history of the tribe. . . . Their
singing is but a succession of grunts and is anything but
agreeable." Thus appeared the first major commentary on
the Navajo Ways in English. One wonders how an educated
observer could possibly have overlooked the intricate ceremonials of a tribe as vast and spiritually complex as the
Navajo. What, then, are the Ways? They are a series of
myths—in diametric contradiction to Dr. Letherman's hy-
pothesis—that describe, fully and well, the origin of the
Navajo tribe.

Each ceremonial myth consists of hundreds of verses of
songs that have been traditionally chanted by medicine men.
Since the Navajo did not have a written language, they
recorded their mythology through a series of ritual songs
that were connected to ceremonies.

The purpose of the ceremony was a curing or healing rite
that was meant to harmonize an individual with his or her
environment. By learning of the past through the Ways, the
individual became one with the present and ensured the
future. This, in itself, was, and is, the basis of Navajo medicine. Well over a hundred years ago, following the blunder
of Dr. Letherman, another visitor to the Navajo, Washington Matthews, learned that all Navajo ceremonials con-

tained the word *hatal*, which means "sacred chant." In one chant alone Dr. Matthews recorded some 576 subsongs or little chants. He also discovered that the Ways themselves were made up of a combination of three things, of which the chant was only one part. The other two parts that were joined to it were the sand painting, a visual, artistic illustration of the chant, and the physical ceremonial, the actual doctoring performed by the medicine man. Together, these three things made up the one Navajo Way.

Long ago, there may have been hundreds of Ways; today, only a few have survived. The best known, the Blessingway, the Moving Up Way, the Flintway, the Holyway, the Featherway, the Waterway, the Windway, the Mountaintop Way, the Beadway, are included in this book.

The story is told on the Navajo Reservation today of the man who got a bad headache while herding sheep. Overcome with pain, he returned to his hogan and told his wife to summon a hand-trembler. The hand-trembler, or diviner, by placing her hands over the body of the patient, received a mystic message that revealed the nature of the illness.

The sheepherder was told that he had accidentally killed a rattlesnake. Snakes are deities to the Navajo and figure importantly in their rituals. The herder, having fallen out of harmony with his world, was now going to be reinducted into it by a medicine man. The ceremony chosen for curing him was the five-day rite known as the Evil-Chasing Way.

Joined by relatives and friends, the herder entered this ritual of well-being, knowing that it would return him to a state of grace within the sacred weft of the Navajo world.

And in five days he was cured.

Hand-tremblers are but one kind of diagnostician on the

Navajo reservation. Another kind, stargazers, use rays of starlight to give them their power. The following is an actual account of the healing way of the stargazer:

> A lamb was given in exchange for the stargazer's services. He knelt down by the young girl who was sick. Then he went out of the hogan very quickly, and looked up into the sky. He stared directly into the starlight. And he began to sing. He kept looking at the star. Then he went back inside the hogan and told the family that there was nothing to be done, for the girl would soon die. In less than a month she was dead. When the stargazer was asked at a later date how he knew the girl was not going to recover, he explained that when he stared into the night sky, he saw a single star that broke open before his eyes. Within this star, he saw a blazing hogan, a sign of death. That was how he knew.

Navajo ceremonies are centered around the belief that harmony—"walking in beauty"—is the most important thing in life. The Blessingway, for instance, used at the birth of a baby, the change from girlhood to womanhood, the blessing of a new hogan, is a cleansing rite that brings psychic wholeness as it also creates a wall of protection around the participants. The primary focus of the more than fifty ceremonial Ways is the maintenance of harmony and balance, the preservation of the essential oneness of the universe. When a man or woman, knowingly or unknowingly, steps out of life's beauty-walk, then illness steps in.

The ceremonies themselves, conducted by a medicine man or woman, are really a sort of verbal reenactment of the Navajo central myth of origin. By merging the patient and his/her family with the holy people—First Man and First Woman, Elder Brother, the Animal People, Sun Father, and Changing Woman—the pattern of harmony is reestablished. This is accomplished, not only by singing and cer-

emony, but also through the rite of the sand painting, a
pageant of colored sand that depicts the deities and brings
the patient into physical proximity with the holy people.
Thus, at the same time he/she is being "sung into health,"
the patient is also receiving the blessing of the deities. It is
as if Zeus or Hera, in the world of the ancient Greeks, had
come from the sky to resolve an earthly or human dilemma.

There are more than fifty Ways used by the Navajo. In all
of them the myths of origin are dramatically present. The
Navajo spirit of self-awareness, a cooperative sense of the
interdependency of all living things, stems directly from
the living morals of the origin myth. Handed down, generation to generation, the myth speaks of the ways in which
the holy people activate life and initiate Dineh, or The
People, into the world of harmony.

Mircea Eliade, the French anthropologist, once wrote:

> Myth narrates a sacred history; it relates an event that took
> place in primordial Time, the fabled time, the "beginnings."
> In other words, myth tells how, through the deeds of Su-
> pernatural Beings, a reality came into existence, be it the
> world of reality, the Cosmos, or only a fragment of real-
> ity—an island, a species of plant, a particular kind of human
> behavior, an institution. Myth, then, is always an account of
> creation. . . . The actors in the myths are Supernatural Be-
> ings. They are known primarily by what they did in the
> transcendent times of the "beginnings." Hence, myths dis-
> close their creative activity and reveal the sacredness (or the
> supernatural) into the World. It is this sudden breakthrough
> of the sacred that really establishes the World, and makes it
> what it is today. Furthermore, it is as a result of the inter-
> vention of Supernatural Beings that man himself is what he
> is today; a mortal, sexed, and cultural being.

The origin myth of the Navajo tells not only where The
People came from, but it further supplies them with a jus-

tification for being. The holy people tell what must be done to have a good life and they explain what can happen if sacred rules are broken. The origin myth occupies the same role in Navajo life as the Bible does in the life of a devout Christian. It informs, and in so doing, it is itself formed in the style or manner of the telling. The origin myth comes from the oral tradition and has been passed down through generations of medicine men and storytellers all the way to the present day. Many versions of the same myth can, and have, been told in different ways, and one is not more "authentic" than another.

Today, as the Navajo tribe faces extreme economic and political pressure, the question arises, especially among the youth, whether there is ultimate value in holding on to the old ways. Some elders of the tribe say that the time has come to resist the pressure from outside the reservation. They say that if the earth, which is the deity Changing Woman, is harmed by the mining of radioactive minerals, then her heart will stop. It is what the environmentalists are saying in the culture at large.

The myths of the Navajo teach us, Indian and non-Indian alike, that when the dreams end, there is no more greatness. When men and women do not know their place, there is no place for them. This is what is happening today. And it is why the old ones sing the old songs so that those who listen might also remember.

Through recitation of the Ways, the Navajo see their world as it was, but also as it will always be. In the beginning, we are told there were no stones, plants, or light. In the First World there was only the beginning of movement as the origin creatures, ants and beetles, went on a journey that would lead to an upper world, or as The People put it, an emergence. With this emergence into an upper world came the appearance of First Man, First Woman, First Boy, First Girl, Fire God, Talking God, Coyote, and the other deities. There was, however, no creator, no Old Testament God pulling order out of the void. Rather the affairs of men, animals, and insects were their own doing, and they negotiated time and space as independent cocreators.

And there was no hierarchy among these crucial early players on the first field of life. From the stirrings of movement, a desire to move upward, to change, arose. Conscious activity, rather than external action, gave presence to life in the First World.

The four worlds of the Navajo correspond to our medieval cosmography of earth, air, fire, and water. In Navajo terms, as well as in present-day scientific interpretation, the First World was one of fire. As the fire (volcanic eruption) cooled, it gave birth to the second world of air. The First World gave man his "life heat," the Second World gave him his "life breath." The Third World of water (condensation of hot vapor) constituted man's internal "water system"—his blood and watery passage system. As the Third World subsided, the fourth emerged, the world of earth, substance, matter. The Fourth World gave man his "earthlife," the flesh of Mother Earth. Together, these four emerging worlds of the Navajo not only gave man his presence, his reality, but they also gave him his geologic history, as depicted in the Ways.

From this, The People and their allies completed a kind of upward journey of the human psyche, learning from each other as they went along. Who were these primary characters?

The main deities of the Navajo pantheon are Sun Father and Earth Mother, who is also known as Mother Earth, or more commonly to the Navajo, Changing Woman. From these two parents came twin sons, or the Hero Twins, known as Monster Slayer, or Elder Brother; and Born of Water, or Younger Brother.

The special attributes of these four major mythological figures govern a complex world made up of a great many subordinate deities, or as they are known to the Navajo, Yei, Holy People. These deities include First Man and First Woman as well as all of the elements of the geophysical realm, which the Navajo have given personal names and familiar identities: Wind, Fire, Water, Rainbow, Thunder, Lightning, and many others. The aspect of holiness, just like the Elizabethan cosmology, penetrates from the highest to the lowest form of matter. All are deemed sacred; all possess life, thought, and independent action. Dust, Worm, Fire Poker are each members of an infinite alliance of beings who, no matter how small, are part of the whole.

Animals, insects, and inanimate objects are equals in the origin stories. Locust, for instance, shot the arrow into the darkness, which opened the way for the next world of light. Turkey carried the sacred seeds of life in his pinfeathers and shook them into the next world of earth, of fecundity. Wind blew life into the unalive Mountains. Each creature, each entity, played its part, making it possible for life to begin in "roundness," in divine accordance. (Please note that at the end of this book there is a glossary of mythological beings, symbols, and terms that will facilitate an understanding of this introduction, as well as subsequent chapters).

One of the most controversial characters among the Navajo is Coyote, prince of chaos, who is also the most notable catalyst. Transformer, troublemaker, trickster, deity—Coyote is all of these, and more. He stole the stars laid out by First Man and scattered them, willy nilly, across the heavens. Yet, from Coyote's unruly behavior, changes came about that made life better. From Coyote's foolishness, mortals gained wisdom, learned what, and what not, to do. Coyote, as the forerunner of change, created ways of doing things so that customs—new moral codes, ceremonies, designs for living—came into being. Coyote's selfish acts thus clarified the boundaries of human and animal conduct.

Acting as the wise fool, Coyote is able to speak and act as others of the holy pantheon, due to inherent decorum, cannot. His role was, and is, a large one. In the literary sense, he is a court jester, moral chorus, and commentator. Indirectly, by unleashing chaos on the world, Coyote brought Changing Woman or Mother Earth into being. The Navajos say that She is the child of Horizontal Woman and Upper Darkness. Once born, Changing Woman matured (some storytellers say it took eighteen days) into a fully grown woman. Her children with Sun Father are the Hero Twins, who are responsible for cleansing the world of monsters, the blood of which is now the hardened lava flows of the desert.

Through the birth of Changing Woman, the emergence into the Fourth and final World becomes complete. With the addition of Changing Woman's beneficent creative power, which is stronger than that of any other deity, life is arranged permanently, order is achieved over the previous worlds of chaos. The Fourth World, the one we live in today, is where the new race of beings were born out of Changing Woman's—Mother Earth's—body. This new race is known as Dineh, The People, The Navajo.

It is difficult in writing of the Ways to separate the myth from its medicinal application, or even the myth from reality. The medicine men who recite the origin story in healing practice do not separate it from the daily life of the patient who is being treated. Instead, it is considered a part of daily living, the bone and breath of the one who has fallen out of harmony. In order to revitalize the patient, the medicine man/singer must return him to a state of cosmological well-being. Anthropologist Gladys Reichard once said: "The singer discussing his belief, as well as the layman asking a direct question, resorts for his answer to myth, which he considers final." The Navajo Ways, then, depend upon the faith that mythological time is the same as historical time, that these two converge, making myth and daily life one. How, otherwise, could a recitation of the myths of The People actually heal them in their hour of need? Consider that a Navajo singer's oral complement of myths may involve hundreds of intricately worded verses. One error in presenting these during a ceremonial could—in the medicine man's mind—cost the patient his life. The deities are made from memory and the depth of this lore is nearly incalculable. In former times, when a medicine man made a mistake in oral recitation, he was honor-bound to quit his practice. In some cases, if his faltering caused a complication in the healing of his patient, or brought about the patient's death, he might actually take his own life.

Navajos do not have a church or a priest to preside over the ceremony. The singular presence of the medicine man is like the role of a priest, but he is also a historian, storyteller, teacher, medical doctor, psychiatrist, and often a diagnostician as well. The medicine man may, therefore, fill the roles of six different functionaries.

How does the medicine man actually heal a patient by reciting a Way? In Navajo terms, the method of returning the patient to a state of grace requires that he or she be placed in spiritual and physical proximity within the holy circle of the deities. This is done through the Ways, combining singing, ceremony, and sand painting. The sand painting that symbolically re-creates the myth brings the patient into physical contact with the deities that rule over a specific illness. The patient sits upon the sacred sand while the medicine man sings the songs of origin. Thus the patient is immersed in the collective unconscious of the tribe, the deepest wellspring of communal faith. Along with the medicine man, the patient is surrounded by family and friends. Over the years, there has been a growing interest in Navajo sand painting, which, according to Mary C. Wheelwright, was not well documented until the mid-twenties and thirties. As she has commented, "Up to recent times there were no copies of sand paintings or other ceremonial designs made in permanent form, the only records being held in the minds of the medicine men."

To appreciate the power generated by a sand painting, one must first visualize the place where the ceremony is held. When held indoors, the ceremony begins in a hogan, the traditional Navajo dwelling. The hogan is built either octagonally, or in the shape of a circle. Older hogans were constructed of mud and log, but today they are fashioned out of almost any usable building material. Traditionally, the roof of the hogan had a smoke hole for the exiting of wood smoke, which was also used to let in light and air. Symbolically, the hogan is representative of an earthen womb, which contains each of the sacred elements: earth, air, fire, and water.

The hogan is built facing east so that it can greet the rising sun. The doorway, whether of blanket or wood, must be tightly closed during the ceremonial. The medicine man sits on a sheepskin or blanket against the western wall of the hogan. During the recitation of the Way, which takes place at night or in the early morning, the patient is asked to sit upon a newly prepared sand painting. The painting is composed of the sacred Navajo colors: red, white, yellow, black,

and blue, with a background of adobe-colored sand. Of
these colors, three of them—red, white, and yellow—orig-
inate in sandstone. Blue is obtained by grinding the charred
root of the rock oak and mixing it with white sand. Black
comes from grinding charcoal with black sand.

After the first blessing of pollen and cornmeal, the patient
removes shoes, clothes, jewelry. The man wears only his
underwear, but the woman removes her shoes, velvet blouse,
and jewelry. The patient is then led by the medicine man to
the sand painting. This is generally west of the painting's
central symbol and always facing east. Thus does the healing ceremony begin.

❦

In the course of the ritual, the medicine man gathers and
presses the holy sand to the body of the patient. This en-
sures that the deities, who have been fashioned ritually and
symbolically out of the sand, will become part of the patient's physical being. In the course of the ceremony, the
following things happen: The sacred colors are painted on
the body; the origin chants are told, sung, heard; the blessing of Mother Earth, in particular, and all the deities, in
general, is felt in the sand itself; Sun Father's light is brought
into the hogan, along with Fire God's; the Hero Twins are
called upon to bless the patient along with the maternal
grandfather figure of The People, Talking God.

Toward the end, when the medicine man has finished his
work and the patient leaves the hogan, the relatives and
friends who have gathered to be a part of the ceremony are
allowed to enter the sand painting from the east, and to
apply the colored sand to their own bodies. From the head
of a deity-design comes the sand that may cure a headache;
from the foot comes the sand that may heal a sprain. When

all have used the sacred sand, the medicine man walks on
the painting, and holding a feather wand in his hand, erases
the symbols. His helpers then put the loose sand into blan-
kets and carry it to the north, where the wind will take it
and pass it around until, once again, it is given back to
Changing Woman, Mother Earth.

Navajos themselves do not catalogue their myths the way
anthropologists do. They live through them and share them,
but they do not normally analyze or systematize them. And
while the Ways combine chanting, singing, sand painting,
and healing practice, their underpinning is the origin myth.
Therefore, it is possible to learn of them, as I have, for
example, primarily in narrative form. My longtime Navajo
friend Jay de Groat knows the Beautyway songs, as well as
the sand paintings, but he believes the heart of the healing
is in the story. For without the legend that links mortal man
to immortal deity, there would be no Way.

The Ways as stories are very much alive today. But, for
the most part, one cannot find them in a book. They must
be heard as part of a living oral tradition. Once, while Jay de
Groat was telling a story, he suddenly looked around ap-
prehensively and said, "I do not want to offend Rattlesnake,
if he is listening."

"That buzzing is just the cicadas," I suggested.

He smiled, but he looked uneasy. The story he told was
invested with life. The moving parts of it were coming together and he believed they were calling a real snake into
our presence. Thus the old expression—"It must be *seen* to be
believed" does not apply here as much as "it must be *heard* to
be believed." The way Jay de Groat learned the stories was
to listen to his father, who is a diviner, a stargazer. "I am

only now beginning to grasp the lessons my father has been teaching me," Jay said recently. And he went on to tell of the Blessingway and how the two men in the myth were not healed properly because "their shadows were weakening them."

I asked what that meant and Jay gave me his father's advice: "Keep an eye on your shadow, don't let it get ahead of you." In case the reader may infer that the message here is Jungian or "New Age," let me hasten to point out the Navajo context. In Navajo mythology, as seen in the Blessingway myth, night is a time of weakening, a time when the shadow is complete. The Sun Father's healing power is not present. Daylight, then, is the time to draw power from the sun; this means to move, literally to "walk in beauty" or harmony with the sun's path in the sky.

Looking after one's shadow, keeping it where it belongs at the appropriate time of day, means simply, being in harmony with oneself, with the Sun Father and the Earth Mother. Jay de Groat's father might well have said—"Follow the sun's path in your daily life, be true to yourself, conscious of where and how you move, and you will be blessed."

The Ways, as I have been hearing them, have come to me from my friends, but primarily Jay de Groat, for the past twenty-fives years. Over time, I have pieced them together from memory and through research, and the result is this book. As much as possible I have tried to keep the oral tradition alive in the stories by not editing the storyteller's voice or his particular style of presentation. The stories are not presented here in their original form as songs or chants because I did not hear them that way; nor did Jay de Groat, for his father told them, a little at a time, whenever a lesson was called for. Here, then, are the lessons of many lifetimes, the Ways that have guided The People from prehistoric time, as they tell it, into the twentieth century.

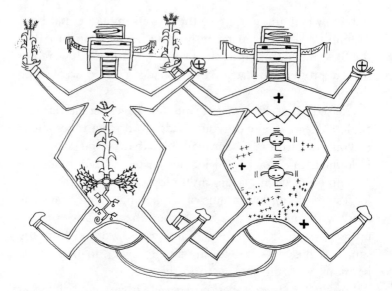

Mother Earth or Changing Woman on left; Father Sky on right. Each is wearing the horns of power; they hold sacred corn plants in their hands and star-crosses. Within Mother Earth, there is a corn plant joined with sacred herbs, and a bird on top. Within Father Sky are the small star-crosses that make up the heavens, and a sun/moon symbol.

THE
BLESSINGWAY

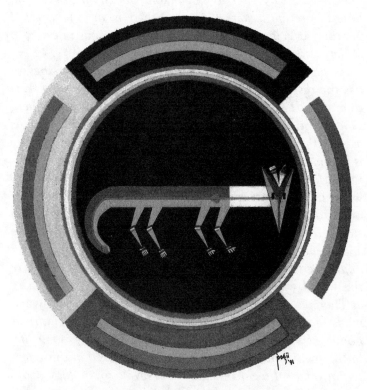

Coyote as depicted by Navajo artist, Jay de Groat. This reproduction of a sand painting was done with colored paper. Note the line, or arrow, that begins on Coyote's nose and ends at the tip of his tail. According to legend, he stores his heart in his tail, and can only be killed by crushing him in that place.

Navajos sometimes call the Blessingway the song of songs, a chant of many parts that contains "all things out of which man is made." The four chants given here, in narrative form, are stories of human and animal conflict and explain how the first people dealt with life, death, and the presence of evil. The storyteller goes back to the beginning of Navajo time to present a stark picture of man as an innocent and uninitiated being, who must call upon the gods in order to understand the world in which he lives.

As perhaps the oldest of all the Ways, the Blessingway has the distinction of being told as often as it is sung. Furthermore, it is frequently given without an accompanying sand painting or prayerstick. Medicine men say that it is used at the start or close of other Ways because its message is seminal to all other forms of healing. What it says, simply, is that life is precious and that man cannot expect to endure without following sacred rules of conduct. Jay de Groat once told me that his father, a medicine man, told him stories from the Blessingway whenever he thought they were applicable to Jay's life. In a similar fashion, a Christian father might recite a passage of Genesis in order to explain the way the world was made and the laws of God that govern it.

There are many individual stories in the Blessingway and medicine men tell them differently to emphasize various points of view. There are also rites of puberty, long life, birth, death, and marriage. The stories offered in this chapter introduce three main figures of Navajo mythology: Coyote, Talking God, and Spider Woman. The reader is confronted with the ancient theme of how we must learn to live in a world that is rife with danger and disorder. In Navajo storytelling style, things happen as they will, in their own way and in their own time. What is given here is one storyteller's answer to the questions that every child has, at one time or another, asked his parents: What is good and evil? What is life? What is death?

Part One of the Blessingway introduces Coyote, the trickster, as a character capable of doing great harm. However, the hoop ceremony, mentioned in the story, reveals how Coyote's evil spell can be remedied.

The hoop ceremonies of the Navajo have been compared by anthropologists to mandalas, Paleolithic sunwheels, or "magic circles." Spruce, willow, and other hoops represent the four passages of man through the four elemental worlds. They are also symbolic of the four directions, the four sacred mountains, the four-cornered construct of the human family—mother, father, son, daughter—and the four stages of human life. By passing through the sacred hoops, symbolically, man reemerges himself, reintegrates himself, immunizes himself. From a weakened state, he passes through the hoops of life into psychological/physiological harmony.

Coyote (think of him as a symbol of chaos) is a clever adversary, but man, in the tale, prevails through the help of Talking God. Known in Navajo as Begochiddy, Talking God is the maternal grandfather of the Navajo. He is a deity like the Greek god Apollo, who often appeared on earth to aid mortals.

In addition to Talking God, man receives spiritual help from a variety of animate and inanimate allies. White Squirrel, for example, is an animate ally, while Fire Poker is an inanimate one. Messenger Fly is a deity who often aids Navajos in distress. The mythic significance of flies and ants in Navajo Ways show that these creatures possess intelligence and wisdom and can be counted on—unless otherwise offended by mortals—as friends.

In Part Two, man journeys into the sky and meets another creature ally, Spider Woman. It is she who makes human arteries, and is thus considered to be a medicine woman. Her spiritual power, as seen in her silken web, joins the realms of Earth and Sky. In most of the Ways, She is a beneficent female, a mother figure who guides mortals and can be trusted to stand up to Coyote when he

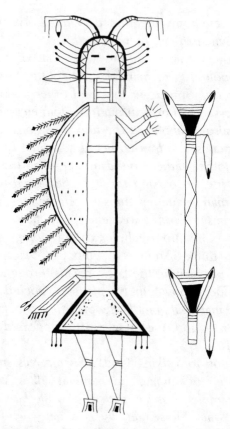

Talking God, maternal grandfather of the Navajo, as shown with ceremonial feathered cane and horns of power.

performs witchcraft or enacts misdeeds. The hoop ceremony is mentioned again in Part Two, as is the sacred
number four, symbolizing the four earthly directions
(north, south, east, and west), the four times of day
(dawn, morning, noon, and night), and the four compo-
nents of family (father, son, mother, daughter).

Breath feathers in the story are prayer feathers, small
downy puffs of the eagle, which Navajos use ceremonially.

In tribal terms, these feathers represent the sacred breath of life. The special power of the breath feather is its ability to float on the wind and, symbolically, carry a mortal prayer up to the spirit world.

Part Three tells the story of the making of day and night, and introduces the animals who contributed to this event. Unlike Genesis, where God divides day and night Himself, in the Blessingway the animals do it themselves by playing the moccasin game. This is basically a kind of hide-the-pea game. In the narrative, Owl is caught cheating, but had he won for his side, night would have dominated day forever. Fortunately, the day animals win, securing equal balance between day and night.

Part Four describes the appearance of two skulls of men slain in battle. In Parts One, Two, and Three we learn that life is sacred and that it must be maintained through harmony and through ceremony. However, in Part Four, we are given the actual story of how life can be nurtured even in the face of death. As in the Christian allegory of Jesus and Lazarus, life can be "breathed" into death. Many of the Yei, the Holy Ones, are called upon to perform the bringing-back-to-life ceremony that is the culminating feature of the Blessingway. The lightning-struck tree is significant because lightning bolts are thrown from the sky by the Sun Father and by Thunder. The power inherent in the bolt is now in the wood of the tree. When the prayer feather of life is pointed at it, the connection is made between Heaven and Earth, deity and mortal, and life is given back to that which was once dead.

PART ONE

Somewhere near the Chaco River there was an Earth Man who went out hunting one day and ran into Coyote. This was unfortunate because, as everyone knows, Coyote is a tricky person. As soon as he saw the Man, Coyote shook his skin over him, and the Man fell to the ground, unconscious.

After he came to, the Man crawled into the hole of White Squirrel. He tried to enter White Squirrel's den three times, but only after the fourth time was he permitted to come in. The Man was sick from Coyote's witchery, so White Squirrel made a hoop of grey willow, fir, and rose bush. He made the Man go through these in the ceremonial way, and the Man felt better but he was still not well.

Then Messenger Fly brought Black Wind and Black Wind used roots of fir and other mountain trees. He put the roots on the Man and broke them over his body, and soon the Man could speak.

While this was happening, Coyote went to the Man's hogan, pretending to be the Man. The Man's wife and his eldest son believed that Coyote was the Man. But the youngest son was not so easily tricked.

Meanwhile, White Squirrel told the Man to go home. On the way the Man heard something speak to him. It was Fire Poker, who told him to go east. So the Man went out toward Farmington, and there met Crow.

"Ha!" Crow said, "You are the one bewitched by Coyote."

The Man agreed.

"Go to the San Juan River," Crow said.

But though the Man knew Crow was a friend of Coyote's, he still went to the river. But he found nothing there.

Then he met Pottery Bowl, who told him to go west.

That brought him no luck. Then he met Buzzard, who told him to go down river. That did no good, but he heard "sh-sh" four times: It was Hair Brush, who told him to go down river farther.

Finally, the Man found his family in the Blue Mountains of Utah. His wife didn't know him and neither did his oldest

Prayerstick.

son, but the younger one knew him. That evening Coyote came home and saw the Man.

"Ah, you've found us," he said. Then, "I need some feathers to make arrows, would you go with me to get some?"

The man agreed to do this. Together, they went to Eagle's nest, which was set up high in a cliff.

"Why don't you go up the rock to the cave first?" the Man said.

"No. You go first," Coyote answered.

So the Man went first.

When he got near the cave, he saw that the young eagles were actually large black locusts. The Man was hanging on a rough piece of rock, trying to get to the cave. The Coyote blew on the rock and it went up into the sky, and the Man was stranded there.

Satisfied, Coyote went home.

Now Messenger Fly saw what happened and he wasn't going to let the Man hang on that rock forever. So he went to look for Talking God.

While he was searching for him, Lightning came and took the Man away.

Talking God went with Elder Brother and Younger Brother to find the Man. Together, they went to the Four Cloud Houses. But they did not find him there. Then they went to the Four Houses of Wind, the Four Houses of Green Slime, the Four Houses of Moss, the Four Houses of Mountain, the Four Houses of Rock, and the Four Houses of Wood. But the Man wasn't in any of the houses. Where was he?

Lightning had him. He took him to Left-Handed Wind, the darkness. He took him to He-Who-Wanders-in-the-Dark, the Darkness Woman, and to the House of Darkness. The Man was watched over by two Dark Guards.

"Who comes?" the Dark Guards said when they heard a noise.

"It is I, Talking God." He had a prayerstick and a stone knife in his right hand and lightning in his left hand.

The Dark Guards moved toward Talking God, but his power was too great and he overcame them at once. Then he woke the Man by pressing a prayerstick to his body, and he gave four prayersticks to the Dark Guards and they hid their heads from him.

Then Talking God took the Man back to his hogan, but he warned him: "When you meet Coyote again, do not allow him to speak first!"

Once in his own hogan, the Man asked his younger son when Coyote was supposed to return. The boy replied that Coyote would come that afternoon. Then the Man told his wife to grind up some seeds and the Rock of Four Colors, and he told her to put them in a line by the fire;

and she knew who he was now and she did the things he asked.

That afternoon when Coyote stepped into the hogan, the Man said right away: "Come and eat these four cakes and I will let you have my family."

"Then I will surely eat the cakes," Coyote said, grinning.

He ate the hot stones the wife had prepared and immediately went running round the fire crying that his belly was on fire. Then he fell down and begged the Man to save him, but the Man would not do it.

"The fur and whiskers that I took off to be a man, I will now put back on," Coyote said. It was the last thing he said and did. He died then. And far off in the desert, the Man heard a coyote wail.

PART TWO

After a time, Uppermost Wind called the Man and brought him to a hogan in the sky. There he met Spider Woman.

"Ah, you have come," she said.

"Yes, I am here."

"Have some of this food," she said.

But Spirit Wind whispered to the man not to take it, and he obeyed.

"Would you like some strawberries?" she asked.

Spirit Wind whispered in his ear, "Eat them, they are good."

And the Man ate the strawberries.

Then Spider Woman offered him some blackberries.

"Those are good too," Spirit Wind said, and added, "This woman will teach you everything." After he ate the blackberries, Spider Woman told the Man that her children had been eaten by wasps.

The Man said, "I will help you." Using his firestick, he lit a bundle of bark and waved it around the hogan four times. This killed all the wasps but four.

To these four, he said: "From now on you will be our friends."

The four wasps said that it would be so.

Spider Woman was grateful to the Man and she blew on her web four times and lowered him down to earth. He then got breath feathers and tied them to her web. She was very pleased with this.

Afterward, Wind taught the Man how to make sacred hoops and he tied breath feathers on the hoops and all was well.

PART THREE

The Day Animals and the Night Animals played a moccasin game that lasted four days.

The Night Animals and Birds had Owl as their leader. The Day Animals and Birds had Coyote as their leader.

Both sides decided the game had to come out a tie, because if one side won, it would be either all night or all day for everyone ever after, and no one wanted that to happen.

So a small stone was hidden in one of the many moccasins of the game.

Nighthawk took first guess, and won.

Then Big Squirrel won.

Then Small Owl.

Then Martin.

Then Bat.

Then Grey Squirrel.

Then Prairie Dog.

Then, the stone got lost.

Gopher and Locust looked underground for it but they could not find the stone.

Then Red Bird struck Owl's hand, and the stone, which Owl had been hiding, dropped out.

And the game was ended as a tie.

PART FOUR

There was a dangerous noise and two white things came rolling out of the desert. The white things were skulls, the heads of two men, twins from Taos.

Talking God and Black Wind went to Taos to find the bodies, but when they found them the bodies were skeletons. Then Fly was told to go to the Black Ant People.

Fly said, "You must collect their flesh and blood."

The Black Ant People did this and they put the collected bodies into a holy buckskin. Spider Woman chewed roots and blew them into the buckskin to make the veins. Talking God then spent twelve days putting the bodies together and making them whole.

The deities were summoned and they came. There was Earth, Lightning, White Corn, Blue Corn, Corn Boy, Many-colored Corn, Deer, Pollen, Man-Rain, Woman-Rain, Water, Black Cloud, Dark Air, Rainbow, Thunder, Sun, Spirit Wind, Small Water, Dawn.

So it was that the men who were once skulls came to life, but they were not well yet.

Fly said, "I know what is wrong: Their shadows weaken them." So the deities made offerings of turquoise, white shell, jet, and abalone, and they pointed a prayer feather at a tree that had been struck by lightning, and they all prayed, and the two men became strong again.

Then Elder Brother healed them with boughs of fir and pine and the Flint Boys healed them with arrows; and Talking God taught the Blessingway to the Earth People; and the Two Brought Back To Life returned to their homes, and lived long and well.

THE
MOVING UP WAY

The Moving Up Way is, overall, a sex-death-transformation myth, which makes harmony out of the discord of human desire. It is a kind of taming of the tempest of human sexual energy, a peacemaking tale that ends in discipline and order. As the storyteller enlarges on the nature of the world—its wild vicissitudes and shifting patterns—he also embroiders a place for man, a place both maternal and beautiful.

The name "moving up way" may be derived from the fact that this Way follows The People's spiritual ascendance as they seek a higher order of evolution. All of the Ways are, in a sense, upward-moving, growing, changing frames of mind and emotion. As they move up from an older and more distant past, The People become more conscious of who they are; this is the purpose of the Way, to instruct the listener in his or her origin.

The story line in the Moving Up Way follows the precarious doings of Coyote as he woos, makes love to, and marries his human girlfriend. In the upsurge of their relationship—much complicated by her disapproving brothers—Coyote is beaten to a pulp by his lover. Every part of him is smashed except the tip of his tail. According to Navajo lore, it is not Coyote's unusual atomic structure that gives him his regenerative gift (like Wily Coyote in the popular cartoon, he is virtually impossible to kill), rather it is his ability to hide his vital parts from harm by storing them in the tip of his tail. Coyote's lover learns his secret and performs it herself later in the story.

Coyote imparts a message which has a positive value for mortal beings: how to protect oneself from physical danger. The Moving Up Way shows us, clearly and well—once we

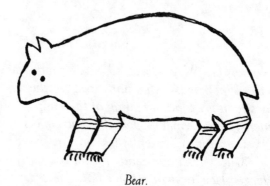

Bear.

understand it—how to remove ourselves from pain by drawing the body/mind into a protective place. On a literal level,
this means extending the threshold of physical pain, but the
Moving Up Way goes beyond this; it protects and heals
those who have encountered a violent act and it helps to
mend broken bones. Medicine men point out that when a
bone is broken, the inner man is "broken off" from the outer
world, which is his outer self. When we see something that
is disruptive because of its inherent violence, we are separated from personal harmony. The medicine man, as well as
the storyteller, seeks to reacquaint us with our true nature,
the integrated self that is beyond disruption; this is the self
of origin, hence, the salve of the origin story.

The main characters in the narrative are Coyote, Coyote's
lover, Bear Woman, and Wind. Bear Woman is especially
significant because she is a person of darkness created by
Coyote's misdeed. By fornicating with a human woman,
Coyote threatens the divine harmony of his world. His
lover, as a result, becomes Changing Bear Maiden or Bear
Woman. There is a definite malign quality to her, which
mortals are taught to guard against. However, as Navajo
storytellers say, Coyote's misdeeds often bring about har-

monic results. After Bear Woman is slain, her body parts are scattered about and they become the lovely images of the natural world. Thus, the Moving Up Way explains that piñon nuts are good to eat because they come from Bear Woman's breasts. And from her limbs come prototypical bears and her intestines give birth to archetypal snakes. All of these are sacred to the Navajo, but without Coyote's misconduct they would not have been born.

Wind is an element, which carries the life-force of nature. In the Ways, Wind is thought to be a messenger who possesses cunning, but also a certain caring for mortals. Medicine men breathe upon their patients to invigorate them with Wind's power, for it was Wind who first gave life to the mountains. In the middle of the Moving Up Way, Little Wind teaches Younger Brother how to stay alive, and at the end of the story, it is Left-handed Wind who helps to recover Coyote's broken body.

PART ONE

At night Coyote lay down opposite the girl, in the corner of the room. It was a cold night and he made a fire, but soon he had burnt up all the wood. Toward dawn he started to inch his way over to the girl.

"Let me just lie at your feet, Sister-in-law," he said, trying to get in good with her. Then he added: "One doesn't always want sex . . . I simply wish to stay warm."

"All right," she said.

But Coyote kept trembling and waking her up.

"Let me just lie with the tip of your blanket over the tip of my nose," he begged. And, again, he addressed her as sister-in-law, and added, "my fellow" to let her know their relationship was a sensible one.

"All right," she said.

But no sooner had she said it, than he pleaded again, his teeth chattering with cold.

"We don't have to have sex, you know," he said reasonably, adding, "Sister-in-law, my fellow," to make certain she understood his intentions were just and honorable. But as she made no move to stop him, he inched up closer and closer—and how his belly showed white as he crept up!

"My, my," he said, "am I ever chilled!"

And he twisted his full length until he was upon her, and he said: "I'll just lie like this with my penis lying on top of it."

And she said, "All right."

"Now I will lie a little closer in."

She did not object. So he moved in, three times.

"All right," she said, "go ahead and do it."

And he did: Four, five, six times.

"Go ahead," she told him.

He said, "Seven, seven, seven, seven—"

Then, "—Ah, I can't count anymore."

Thus they both lost count, and in the morning, she who had refused all others had become the wife of one who was the worst of all. She who was so fine had made Coyote her husband.

As it happened, the girl's brothers, twelve of them, disliked the smell of Coyote's urine around the hogan, so they moved out, setting up their own hogan nearby. One day when they all went hunting, he asked to come along and they said all right. But as the hunt began, Coyote promised to drive the animals to the brothers.

"Turn them in our direction," they said.

He did this, and when a mountain sheep was killed, Coyote rushed in and claimed the horn, even though this was the right of the one who had shot it with an arrow.

"The fat of the horn is mine, Relations-in-law," Coyote said.

Four times he claimed the fat of the horn and four times the brothers said no. Later on, as they were carrying the bags of meat home with them, Coyote was warned not to sit down until the meat was brought back to their hogans. He agreed as they started off, but soon he got tired and put his load down. When he picked it up again, it seemed heavier than before. Then, each time he rested, the load got heavier until, in the end, it was too heavy for him to do anything but drag it along. Then he even got tired of doing this and began to decorate the trees with the meat. What remained in the bag, he left to spoil in the sun.

After a while, walking along, he came to Slim Water Canyon. He saw some Spider People there and called out to them: "Hey, how is it your wives are so ugly?" They didn't answer, so he said: "Why is it your teeth stick out?" They still didn't answer, so he said: "My wife is really beautiful!"

Then they answered, "Get away Coyote, First Scolder. Don't turn this place into your pisspot!"

"Hmm" Coyote hummed. "First Scolder, is it?"

"You heard us, Roamer and Scolder!" they shouted.

"So he roams and scolds, does he?" Coyote mumbled under his breath. He was getting angry, letting it build up into a hot fire inside him.

Then he called out, answering them: "Fact is, I do things for your benefit. Not for me—for you!" But by then they had heard enough of him. Spider Man and Spider Woman had both made a few webs to catch him up. Coyote ran at the webs and broke through easily—one, two, three—but the fourth time, they got him. And they killed him and cut up his hide and spread it around so that even Swallow got a strip of it: That is the white streak you see on Swallow today.

When the twelve brothers got back to their hogans with the meat, their sister, Coyote's wife, was waiting for them. "Where is he who went with you?" she asked.

"He was right behind us," one of them said.

"You must have killed him," she said. "I know how you hated his smell."

"No, it isn't that way," one said. "He was just behind us, carrying his heavy pack of meat."

"You hate him!" she said again.

But they insisted he was back there somewhere on the trail.

PART TWO

Now on the east side there is a mountain, a small mountain where dawn comes. Now her growling can be heard, with her hands of fur from the wrists going up. With a deer-bone awl she makes herself a set of teeth. She buries her heart, her veins, her breath, her blood: All these she puts into the earth. Now she is safe, for she learned this from her husband, Coyote. With her blood, her breath, her heart, her nerves, her secret life-breath buried away in the earth, she is safe from harm. Her husband, Coyote, taught her that. But when the Swift People see she is a bear, they come after her and shoot her full of arrows.

Now she sings her song:

> I am Changing Bear Woman.
> To the Monsters, I go.
> The Swift arrows work loose.
> The power from them falls.
> The Monsters, to them, I go.
> Go la, go he.

When the sun rose, she was all bear fur, from the shoulder down. And when her twelve brothers saw her, a fine big, fur bear, they shrank back in fear. The eldest brother then hid the youngest in the hogan. He dug a hole under the fireplace, and buried him there, with food and water and a small air hole so he could breathe. Then the eleven brothers set off, hoping she wouldn't follow them. "Maybe she will spare us," the eldest said.

Soon they split up. The oldest went east; the next eldest went south; the next west; and the next north. But she tracked them down, one after another, and tore them to pieces, bit by bit.

On top of a little hill, she thought of the youngest brother whom she had not yet killed. "Where my urine flies," she said, "I will find Younger Brother." And she peed, and found him.

But Little Wind then rushed into the folds of Younger Brother's ear and told him where his sister, Bear Woman, had hidden her heart and blood and body parts. "Come here," she coaxed, "and I will comb the lice out of your hair."

She said this soothingly, as a sister not as a bear. But Little Wind again crept into the folds of Younger Brother's ear.

"At the white rock, under the oak tree," Little Wind said, "she hides her life. You can see it there, dancing and singing: 'ts-os, ts-os, ts-os, ts-os.' "

Younger Brother listened and Little Wind repeated the warning: "She will kill you as she has killed your brothers. You must shoot down her heart."

Now, when Bear Woman changed back into Younger Brother's sister, she looked as she always did. And when she began combing the lice out of his hair with her fingers, she couldn't help herself: The lice looked so good to eat, her lips turned back into bear's lips, and her fangs came out and ate the sweet lice.

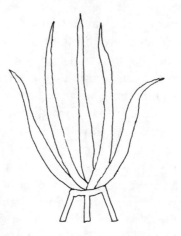

Yucca.

"What are you doing?" Younger Brother asked.

"I am combing the lice out of your hair," she answered.

"What now?" he asked, looking carefully at her shadow.

"Still combing and killing," she answered.

And he saw her shadow lips grow wet and large, and he watched the bear's teeth grow long and sharp. She is still a bear, he thought. Then, while she was busy eating a louse, he suddenly jumped up and ran to the oak tree and saw her heart dancing there, and steadying his arrow, he shot the heart through the center.

"Little Brother, what are you doing?" Bear Woman gasped.

"I am killing you," he said.

"Ahh, ahh," she whispered faintly, dying.

Then he drew a zigzag in the sand, then a straight line; then another zigzag and another straight line. This was done so that her blood couldn't run together and make her well again. After he was sure she was dead, he went to her body and saw that she had changed back into his sister. He took out his knife and cut the place between her legs off.

"Is this the thing that makes men so wild?" he asked.

He threw it into the air and it landed on a yucca tree and from the inside of the yucca a new fruit grew that was good to eat. Then he cut off her breasts and threw them into a piñon tree and sweet nuts grew that were good to eat. Then he cut off one of her arms and threw it to the east, and a black bear walked out of there. The other arm he cut off and threw to the south and a blue bear walked out of there. He cut off one of her legs and threw it to the west and a yellow bear walked out of there. Then he cut off the other leg and threw it to the north and a white bear came out of there. From her intestines came snakes and from her colon came the horned rattlesnake.

After Younger Brother had done these things, he went looking for his other brothers, but they were dead and scattered to the winds. So he asked the help of the Rock Crystal People. With their help he spread out the skin of a deer not killed by an arrow and the brought-together body parts were made whole again, and the brothers were brought back to life.

In time, so they say, Spotted Thunder, Left-Handed Thunder, and Left-Handed Wind went out and found First Scolder. He was no good to anyone broken up into so many pieces, so they put him back together again, and as usual, gave him another chance to be good. Of course, no matter how many chances you give Coyote, he is going to do what he does best: make tricks and mischief, and cause the world to change . . . some say, for the better.

THE
FLINTWAY

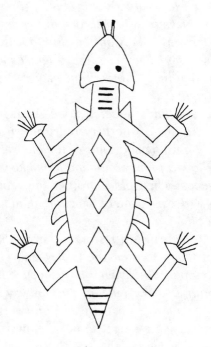

Gila Monster.

W hen a storyteller tells the Flintway, his mind returns to the forgotten days when Gila Monster was the first medicine man. If the storyteller happens to be a medicine man, he may, at the outset of the tale, open up his pouch, full of sacred pollen, and sprinkle some around the four directions. When he does this, he is especially mindful of Gila Monster. For not only is this a medicine story particularly suited to Gila Monster's divining power, but it is also a "myth of armor," of covering the body with a protective shield, of which Gila Monster with his hard scales is considered the best and most exemplary veteran. He is the well-armored warrior of the Navajo. When abroad in the desert, crawling around his domain, Gila Monster's forefoot trembles as he walks. Navajos say that he is the original hand-trembler, which means that he can foretell the nature of mortal illness and protect against it.

To the Navajo, flint is a sacred stone. Arrowheads are said to resemble the tips of the fiery bolt thrown by Thunder. Arrows equal lightning and some of the old warrior tales tell of mortals who wear flint armor and look like Gila Monster. In other legends, when Elder Brother sings flint songs, his voice jingles with the sound of blue flint, thunder flint, water flint, talking flint.

The Flintway, then, is a restorative story that celebrates the power of Gila Monster, the healer, and Flint, the protector. By wrapping the listener in protective bands of legendary strength, the storyteller of the Flintway heals injuries that are the result of torn flesh and broken bone. Other virtues of the story are that it shows the mystic parameters of territory—what land is off-limits to mortals, and which gods command honor there. The Flintway further delineates Navajo obeisance to the life cycles of weather, plant, animal, and reptile. If Man is to "walk in beauty," as the Navajos say, then it is necessary to know what realms are sacred and how to protect mortal flesh and bone when entering an undiscovered country.

Frank Waters states that in the Flintway "the shattered body of the adulterous hero finds its exact parallels in the ancient Greek and Egyptian mysteries." He goes on to say that Apollo is charged by Zeus to gather up the scattered parts of Dionysus-Zagreus who has been slain and dismembered by his brethren.

In the Flintway myth, the hero Elder Brother enters the sacred precinct of Earth Whirling, one of the spiritual centers of the Navajo emergence saga. As the "place was forbidden to enter," White Thunder pummeled him with Lightning, shattering him. Part One, then, establishes the hero's dilemma—entering an off-limits zone of the gods, a place of allegorical dimension. In Part Two, Gila Monster, the healer, sings five major healing songs to restore Elder Brother. These songs are Song of the Black Ant, Song of Thunder, the Sun's Healing Song, Song of the Sun and the Wind, and Song of the Spider Web. Collectively, the songs weave together the loose strands of Elder Brother's shattered self. Black Ant carries "the finest, littlest, tiniest part of the broken-apart man"; Thunder, Lightning, and Rainbow "perfect him"; the Sun and Wind give him "mind and walking power"; Spider weaves "his happiness walking, hanging, glittering." Thus is Elder Brother brought back to life.

PART ONE

One day Elder Brother came upon the track of a deer by the La Plata Mountains. This happened at the time that the months of June and July meet, in midsummer. And it happened at the place called Earth Whirling, a mesa.

He had tracked the deer there at midday, when it suddenly started to rain. Leaning his quiver against a spruce tree, Elder Brother crawled under the boughs to keep dry. But this place was forbidden to enter, and so White Thunder threw Lightning upon the tree and shattered Elder Brother. His arrows were also hit, and they floated off the mesa top.

After one day, Talking God appeared.

"Who is there who knows of this thing?" he asked the Holy People who had gathered.

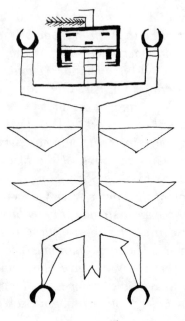

Messenger Fly.

Big Fly said, "He was shattered yesterday by White Thunder."

"Who can help us put him together?" Talking God asked.

"Old Man Gila Monster who lives at the bottom of Earth Whirling—but don't tell him I said so," Big Fly said.

So Wind took a bundle of buckskin to the old man and asked him to make some medicine. The bundle was at the old man's foot, but he made no effort to pick it up. Wind went away and told Talking God: "It seems he has no intention of helping us."

"Give him two buckskins then."

It was done. But the old man lay there with his foot resting on his knee, and made no move to pick up the two buckskins. A third was given to him, and he opened his eye

a crack and said: "What do I know? I don't know a thing."
So Wind left and went back to Talking God.

"Give him four bundles then."

But when he saw the fourth bundle, the old man said:
"Didn't I just tell you I don't know a thing? Get out of here
and leave me alone."

Then Wind was instructed to bring him an unwounded
buckskin with a prayerstick. Mountain Tobacco, Water Tobacco, and Cloud Tobacco were put into it, and pollen was
sprinkled at the top.

Big Fly explained to Wind the correct way of presenting
these sacred things to Old Man Gila Monster.

"Take the prayerstick and move it from the tip of his foot
upward, and around and across his forehead, so, then down
his left side. Then put the prayerstick by his left foot. But,
whatever you do, make sure you don't tell him that I am the
one who told you this!"

So Wind did what he was told to do, moving the prayerstick in sunwise fashion. The old man followed it with his
eyes, around his forehead and down the left side to his foot.
He seemed troubled by something.

Big Fly, who happened to be the guard of the old man's
cave, was sitting nearby.

"Did you tell this person to do this?" Old Man Gila Monster said hoarsely.

"You always accuse me of things!" Big Fly said, trying to
sound offended.

"Who else knows my ways?" the old man whispered drily.

However, in the end, he gave in and took the prayerstick
and the sacred tobacco. The tobacco went into a pipe of jet,
which he raised toward the sun. He drew on it four times
and smoke rose up. He blew smoke upon the earth and then
into the sky. He did this four times.

Then he opened his agate medicine pouch, alive with

breath, and began to cut himself up with a flint knife. He cut
himself to ribbons and then he made himself whole again.
His medicine was very powerful: black medicine, white medicine, blue medicine, yellow medicine, glittering medicine,
dew-drop medicine, cool medicine, red medicine, and mixed
medicine.

PART TWO

He sang, then, the Song of the Black Ant:

> Black Ant People, by your sense of smell, go out and
> put back together this severed body; these are the feet,
> these are the toes, put them in place.
> Here is the ankle, put it in place. Here is the knee, put
> it in place, here is the thigh, put it in place.
> Black Ant People, sing this song, praying and singing and
> doing their work, carrying the finest, littlest, tiniest
> part of the broken-apart man.
> Black Ant People, bring to me his body hair, his blood vein,
> bring every part of him back, by your sense of smell, go out
> and put together this severed body so that we may see him
> whole once again.

And he sang, after this, the Song of Thunder:

> Thunder toward him rose, toward him rose.
> Zigzag lightning into his mouth,
> Thunder toward him rose.
> Rainbow toward him rose.
> Now white medicine, living medicine
> Perfect again it has made you.
> Happiness into his mouth
> Whole again it has made you.

Now it lifts up
Now it puts you up
Now it walks you
Now it trots you
Now it slows you
Now it draws you
Now it makes you
Now it perfects you.

Then he sang the Sun's Healing Song:

Sun looking down on me from above.
Moon looking.
Mountain Woman looking.
Happiness looking.
All that is around, looking.
My surroundings looking.
Now Sun
Now Moon
Now Mountain Woman
Now Happiness
Looking down on me.

And he sang the Song of the Sun and the Wind:

When the man winks but cannot talk, let Wind restore
his walking power
Black Wind under the feet, White Wind under his legs,
Blue Wind under his body, Yellow Wind under his mind,
Glittering Wind under his head (Sun gone under his eyes)
Whirlwind gone under
his walking power.
Black Wind makes the feet whole
White Wind makes the legs whole
Blue Wind makes the body whole
Yellow Wind makes the mind whole

> *Glittering Wind makes the head whole*
> *Sun makes the eyes whole*
> *Whirlwind makes the walking power whole.*

Finally he sang the Song of the Spider Web:

> *On the web of his walking, white medicine,*
> *She of the Spider People makes one perfect again.*
> *On happiness he is walking, blue spider,*
> *Blue web, glittering spider, glittering web.*
> *On the web of walking and hanging.*
> *He of the Spider People starts him off*
> *On a walk; glitter weaver, glitter web, white blue*
> *Black spider web of wellness made,*
> *His happiness walking, hanging, glittering*
> *Webbing body made of wellness, heal.*

And the singing of these songs by Old Man Gila Monster made Elder Brother well again because now he knew how it was done, and how it would be done again in time. And he who had been struck down by White Thunder was returned to himself, and The People saw that what worked for him would work for them. They remembered to honor White Thunder and not go where they were not supposed to go. They remembered to honor Lightning and Wind and give praise to the old man who lived at the bottom of the hill. And they did not forget the way Talking God cared for them or the way Big Fly would see two ways to help a friend. And they remembered that the flint arrows that were scattered were later returned and the body broken up was made well.

They remembered.

THE
HOLYWAY

There is a general feeling among Navajos that several chants may serve the same purpose. There are a number of stories, for instance, that deal directly with attack, and the removal of the effects of attacks, from the Navajo deities Thunder, Wind, Bear, Snake, and Ant. These story-chants are generally known as the Holyway. Their effect is not merely to help the patient, but to placate the gods or, as the Navajos usually call them, Holy People.

How does one offend a god? Medicine men say that a conscious or unconscious offense has been made when a mortal transgresses against the territory of a deity. He may forget to say a prayer when crossing a sacred boundary or accidentally kill an ant, for example. Because of their relationship to mortals in the first emergence stories, all ants are considered symbols of divinity, representatives of the earlier ant deities who helped mortals get out of the darkness of primary existence.

As a central figure of importance in the Holyway, ants, in general, are regarded as highly evolved beings. The Holyway, then, may be used to heal the effects of inadvertently swallowing, or nearly swallowing, these insects. It may also be applicable when ants have been accidentally urinated upon, spat upon, slept upon, or otherwise disturbed by human contact. In addition to ants, the Holyway is used to counteract offenses that have been directed toward other entities or, in Navajo terms, Holy People: Thunder, Lightning, Wind, Bear, Snake, and Horned Toad all fall under the jurisdiction of this Way.

Of the above, perhaps Horned Toad is the most vital. For it was he who was designated as Guardian of the Corn, which is the physical and spiritual food of the Navajo. Fur-

Corn symbol representing the Navajo Tree of Life. Two ears joined suggest physical and spiritual life. The plant depicted here is blessed by Lightning, Rainbow, Rain, and Bird. It gives forth sacred pollen and meal.

ther, Horned Toad is dependent upon ants for his main source of nourishment. All four are vitally bound in this myth: man, corn, horned toad, ant. As an environmentalist would tell us, these four are a kind of paradigm for co-existence in nature; they must, somehow, learn to live together. The Navajos have solved the dilemma of natural balance by enlisting three of these dependents as deities, folk heroes; and they have invented a tapestry of folklore in the Holyway to express the simple and unavoidable truth of synchrony. This, primarily, is what the Holyway is about.

In Parts Two and Three of the Holyway, human problems
of coexistence begin to occur between the sexes. Men and
women have not been given adequate roles to fulfill as yet,
and the result is chaotic. In order to arrive at the next level
of existence, they must work through their selfish ways. The
society, at this point, would appear to be neither paternal
nor maternal, but it tends toward maleness. To relieve this
situation, Old Grandmother Ant Person enters the tale. She
is a male/female role model, and it is through her that the
first men and women of this darkened world of primeval life
begin to know each other and the work they must perform
in order to live together.

Much has been said already about Coyote's contribution
to chaos; Part Four of the Holyway shows Coyote con-
founding order and creating disorder. It is through him that
the Great Flood comes, which, at first, is quite threatening
to human and animal alike. Then, as in other myths, Coyote
is again proven to be a catalyst. By forcing the floodwaters
to rise (Coyote makes this happen by stealing Water Monster's babies) the step up into the next level of existence is
accomplished, and Coyote gets, first the discredit, then the
credit for it. The stage is thus dramatically set for the Featherway, which follows after the Holyway.

It may be observed that the First World of the Holyway
differs from other First World stories. This is because storytellers accept different options and emphasize varying
points of view in their recitations. In some versions of the
origin story the Creator, a kind of unmoved mover, may be
hinted at; in others the Creator is not present at all. In the
Holyway, the myth begins with Water Woman. We are not
told, however, how she came to be, or whether Fire (the
geophysical "first world") preceded her.

Once, in hearing two conflicting presentations of the
same origin tale, I asked why they were not the same. The

answer, according to one storyteller, was that "not everyone has the same mind, or the same thought." I have also heard it said: "Not everyone who listens hears the same words."

PART ONE

In the First World, everything was dark and calm. There was only Water Woman, the Mother. But she thought there ought to be other things beside herself, so she made Earth and Sky, who were twins. Together, Earth and Sky made Black Belted Mountain, Turquoise Mountain, Colored Cloud Mountain, and Big Sheep Mountain.

Horned Toad, Guardian of Corn, shown with protective flint armor and lightning guardian arrows.

When the mountains were made, there was still no life. So
Earth made Black God, who is also known as Fire. Then she
made Horned Toad, Locust, and Blue Lizard. After that she
made First Man and First Woman. From them came the rest
of The People.

However, there was no life in anything. This was because
the beings were empty. Wind had not been born yet, so
there was no life. So it was that things waited. They waited
for strength. While they were doing this, a cloud of light
appeared in the east. It rose and fell and streamers of light
came off it.

The People watched it turn black. From that blackness,
they saw Black Wind coming.

Then the cloud of light turned blue, and Blue Wind came.
The cloud of light turned yellow and Yellow Wind came.
The cloud of light turned white, and White Wind came.
And the cloud of light then showed all colors at the same
time and Many-Colored Wind came.

> *The cloud of light made Rainbow of the Earth.*
> *And there was White Early Dawn*
> *Blue Sky of Noon*
> *Yellow Sky of Sunset*
> *And Dark Sky of Night.*

Each of these times is a holy time of day, and The People
understood this, and when the Winds came and passed
through them, they knew they were blessed. The Winds
made lines on the fingers and toes and heads of The People.
And they entered into the mountains and waters, and everything else. And they gave them life, because Wind is
Creation's first food.

Then Earth made a mountain to the south. It was long and
striped and of different colors: black, red, yellow, and red

and black at the south end. And Earth also made ants, but these she kept underground, until the mountain was ready for them to live in.

From the mountain came the ants of different colors: red, yellow, black, and two-colors. The Big Red Ant People had black plumes on their heads and each carried a black hoop tied with white cotton. There were also Small Red Ant People and Small Yellow Ant People, and they also carried plumes and hoops.

It happened that the Ant People wanted to know what they should eat. So they asked First Man and First Woman: "What do you eat?"

"We eat food that Earth gives us," First Man said. "What do you eat?"

"We eat only Earth," one of the twelve Ant People said.

"That you should not do," First Man said. "You should eat something else."

Then the Five Wind People came from the clouds and offered seeds and plants. The Ant People took them and were thankful. Then, satisfied, the Ant People went back to their mountain.

Sometime after this, the Ant People returned to the place where they had first found their food, that which was Earth. There they saw Horned Toad for the first time. He saw them and ate them.

After he had eaten four of them, an Ant Person asked him why he did this thing.

"I can't help it," he said.

"Why can't you help it?" he asked.

"Because," said Horned Toad, "You are my food."

The Ant People went back to the way they were living. There were many of them, too many of them, and they were quarreling among themselves, biting off each other's heads and legs.

"You see," Horned Toad explained, "That is why I eat you. But even though I do this, you will always live, as long as Earth remains."

However, at this time, life was not really thriving anywhere. The only food was coming from the Wind People, and the Ant People were getting reckless with their fighting. Earth saw what they were doing and She grew tired of it. Then Black God [Fire] began to burn the earth at the four corners. All beings were then driven to the center of the earth where First Man and First Woman, the Wind People, and the Cloud of Light were gathered.

PART TWO

Then it was that they moved upward, leaving the dark world behind. They climbed on top of the Four Mountains, which grew upward with them, and they all moved up into a lighter world. The Wind People brought seeds into the new world, and they planted them:

> To the east, at White Mountain
> To the south, at Blue Mountain
> To the west, at Yellow Mountain
> To the north, at Black Mountain

It was known about then that First Man was the spirit of White Corn. First Woman was the spirit of Yellow Corn. Their children also had spirit life within them and their names were Boy Blue Corn and Girl Many-Colored Corn. Together, these four decided how the earth should be divided.

The Hunters were sent to the White Mountain in the east. There they would live in the place where the only light of this world was. The Planters stayed in the center of the earth, near the Place of Crossed Rivers, where the Male River and the Female River met.

Now the time had come when First Boy and First Girl were the ones who made the rules for this new world. No one knew how it happened, but First Girl had a daughter, and when this one grew up, First Boy married her and they lived together.

But things were not always well. One day First Boy's wife felt sick and asked to be carried to the Place of Crossed Rivers. She said this place made her feel better. So he took her there, and waited and watched, just out of sight. His wife talked to the river. Soon a tumbleweed came tumbling up to her. He saw a man hiding underneath it.

After this, First Boy stopped talking. He was always a great speechmaker, so when he closed his mouth and wouldn't talk, the Ant People worried about him. Finally, a wise Ant Person told him it was time to visit their old grandmother, the Ant Person who was a man dressed as a woman. First Boy visited him and asked him questions:

"How do you get your corn?" he asked.

"I plant it," Old Grandmother said.

"How do you get your meat?"

"I hunt it."

First Boy asked, "How do you get your pottery?"

Old Grandmother answered, "I make it."

"How do you get your cornmeal?"

"I grind it."

"What do you grind it with?" First Boy asked.

"With a grindstone," Old Grandmother replied.

The questions came and were answered wisely, for Old Ant Person was wise and knew many things.

First Boy thought about these things and then he said, "Well, if you can do all this, then so can I."

Then he asked Old Grandmother to help him.

"Tomorrow help The People make a raft of crossed logs. Tie them together with yucca. Then make a smooth platform of logs on top of the raft and put all the male children upon it."

"What do you want me to do with them?" Old Grandmother asked.

"I would like to ask you to float them across the river," First Boy said.

"Very well, Grandson, I will do as you ask."

The next morning Old Grandmother showed The People how to make the raft out of cottonwood and pine. They all gathered at the Place of Crossed Rivers to make the raft.

When the raft was done, the male children were put on top of it. They were all male animal children. This separation by the river made the woman laugh. Later on, a male child was born on the female side of the river, and this child was ferried across by Old Grandmother. But it was the last one.

After this, the women lived their lives on their side of the river and the men on theirs. They did not cross over. At first, the women made much laughter, they laughed out loud at the way the men and children left them. The men, however, did not laugh. They set to work, hunting. They hunted as they were accustomed, toward White Mountain. There was plenty of game for them to eat and make clothing out of.

Time passed, and more time.

At the end of twelve years, the women, who did not plant much food, had only very small plantings to tend. They were hungry most of the time and their clothes were worn out. Across the river they could see the men's garden. It was full of corn, beans, and squash. And the men were dressed well in clothes of buckskin. The women were cold and hungry.

So it came about, after all this time, that First Boy's wife, who had been unfaithful, apologized to him. It was at that time that all the women crossed over, and things were once again well between them. The men made the women new clothes of buckskin and they fed them meat and corn. The men and women made love and they had children.

And everything was peaceful.

PART THREE

The world was not very light. There was no sun, moon, or stars. Coyote was always present, poking his nose into things. One day he saw something pretty flashing in the river.

"I want those things that are floating there," he remarked to Heron. He was looking at two of Water Monster's children who were floating in the river like leaves. He liked them but he didn't know what they were.

"What are they?" Heron asked.

"I don't know," Coyote answered, "but they are pretty, and I want them."

So Heron dived into the water and the pretty things went closer to shore, and Coyote grabbed them, put them under his arm, and went on his way.

Then came the Great Flood. It happened like this:

There was no sun, moon, or stars. In the east, White Dawn, four fingers big, came every morning and at midday, Blue Dawn lit up the south. When late afternoon came, Yellow Dawn streaked the west.

First Boy had asked Coyote to find out the source of the dawn, but instead he stole the two pretty things, which were Water Monster's babies. Time passed, and four finger high White Dawn was only three fingers high streaked with dark.

First Boy asked Wolfman to go out and see what was going on, but when he returned at nightfall, all he said was, "All is well." The next morning White Dawn was very narrow, and the dark streak was bigger still.

Then First Boy sent out Mountain Lion to go out and see what was going on, but all he said was, "All is well." And the dark streak was bigger still.

White Hawk went out to see what was going on, and Sparrow Hawk followed after. White Hawk said: "All is well." But Sparrow Hawk explained that the Great Flood was getting worse and the streak was now a belt of darkness that covered all, and still the water rose.

Now the Animal People gathered up corn and seeds and they climbed:

White Mountain in the east
Blue Mountain in the south
Yellow Mountain in the west
Black Mountain in the north

And the mountains were swallowed up with water, all but one, Black Mountain. So the Animal People planted a female reed in the west and a male reed in the east, and as the water rose, they climbed into the reeds.

Turkey was the last to squeeze into the reed, and the foamy water whitened the tips of his tailfeathers (they are white to this day), and the reeds sprang into the sky and met at the top and went no farther.

PART FOUR

First Boy asked Locust to do something. Locust took his bow of darkness and shot an arrow into the sky, and the arrow tore a hole into the world above, but this world was still water. Locust was the first one through. He saw a Black Bird fly toward him from the east: "How is it you live here?" he asked.

The Black Bird was carrying arrows in his mouth, and said: "Can you do this? If you can, you can live here." And the Black Bird thrust an arrow into his mouth and down his throat.

Locust then stuck one of his arrows through his right side and another through his left side. And the Black Bird vowed that he and the other Animal People could live in that world.

The Animal People were still blocked up in the hole in the reed that Locust had slipped through, and they didn't know what to do. Badger offered to dig them out, and with his large claws he enlarged the hole, and the Animal People got out.

Then the Wind People went up. They broke the dark streaks that made the water flow, and it began to flow off the earth. The Wind People stayed and tamped the ground for four days. Badger came up, then, and asked to help. He dug through the White Earth and it got daubed on his face (it is white-striped to this day). But on the way back down, he got stuck in some black mud (his legs and belly are mud-colored to this day).

First Man and First Woman, First Boy and First Girl, and all the rest of the Animal People came up to the new world. Horned Toad came up and so did the Ant People, which he started at once to eat. The only ones he did not eat were the Yellow Ant People, because they came up last (they come out now only at night, so he can't eat them), and Horned Toad said a prayer in exchange for his food.

After this, all the Animal People came up. Lion, Deer, Antelope (these are now the Pueblo people, the Ute people,

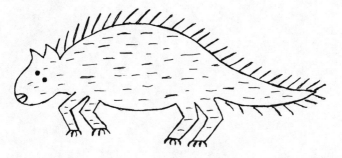

Badger.

and the Apache people) also came. Two people who came up had arrows in their hands: One went to the sun and the other went to the moon. There were four white-faced people who came up (these are the White people of today) and they were riding upon a rainbow. They went away, but they said they would return one day and teach what they knew to the others.

The new world was a good place to live. However, the water still flowed from the Great Flood and made it too wet to live. The Animal People discovered that Coyote had kept the two pretty things under his arm. These were the Water Monster babies whose theft had caused the Great Flood. So First Man made Coyote return them to their mother, Water Monster.

After that, the water went down.

And all was well.

THE
FEATHERWAY

The Featherway begins in darkness and leads upward into the light. The power of healing as felt in this Way comes through the breath feather. Whereas the breath of life as exemplified in feather symbols is mentioned in the other Ways, in the Featherway its use is demonstrated. The story-teller, through his recitation, imparts the message that breath is the true element of life. In the manner of his telling it, by breathing deeply and frequently pausing, as if to hold his breath, the power of the Way is emphasized by the Navajo storyteller.

The medicine man uses breath feathers in his application as well. He might, for instance, touch the patient with a feather on the head, or around the places where the patient is ailing. The Featherway is usually employed to treat head illnesses—particularly deafness and blindness. It is also used, however, to treat paralysis and rheumatism. Eye infection and resultant blindness once plagued the Navajos during the 1800s and the Featherway may have been used against it, but the Way was not created for this reason.

The setting of the Featherway symbolizes the theme of the world of darkness that must be overcome. And that is just what happens in the story. Also in the tale is the implicit fact that animals and men—all living creatures—have not yet learned to reach beyond instinctual reasoning; therefore, in a symbolic sense, they are deaf to the world they live in. The darkness that they inhabit seems to be one of their own making, for they are blind to the inseparability of man and woman whose virtues, like day and night in the Blessingway, must be equal partners. Thus the characters in the Feather-way exist very much in a dream world where light cannot penetrate because The People are unable, or unwilling, to see the truth.

One of the main characters in the Featherway is Shapeshifter, a character common to North American tribes, who is a mysterious deity who can shape himself into any form that suits him. In this story he commits adultery, but is not caught. A friend of Coyote, living outside the law of the tribe, Shapeshifter moves in darkness. Yet his acts have positive effects and bring about affirmative things. As part of the healing transition of the myth, he is brought into the communal, tribal world and given an assignment: to watch over and be responsible for game animals. Coyote is also given a definite role: guardian of wind, rain, and childbirth. First Woman Chief makes her appearance as a wise counselor, first proof that The People can and will be governed by female consciousness; in other words, the society in the Featherway is beginning to grow matrilineally.

Other, deeper societal values are also established in the myth. Death is brought into being, time is positioned in the heavens. Light is given to the constellations. First Man and First Woman are accorded special powers of governance; although deities, they are startlingly human, sexed, and mortal-seeming figures.

The plot of the Featherway revolves around the first assignments given to human and animal personages in the emergence myth-drama. In Part One, we find out why snakes haven't any arms or legs; how the stars were made to shine; how infidelity was cured; and we are told of the birth of the Hero Twins, Monster Slayer and his brother, Born of Water. Part Two describes the journey taken by the Sun's son. This story is variously told; in some versions it is Born of Water who makes the journey and in others (this one, for instance), it is described as "another boy who was born at a

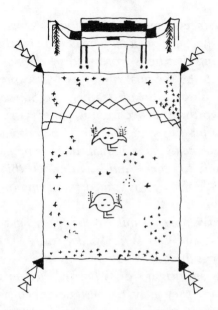

Sun Father with Sun and Moon symbols within him; also depicted are
Star-crosses to indicate the heavens.

place called Zuni." The journey itself is rendered here partly
in poetry form because that is the identification that I caught
in the storyteller's voice, a rhythmic chanting. Poetry often
enters into a tale when, as Jay de Groat explains: "A pause in
the hero's journey is interrupted by some natural cause—a
steep mountain, a river—a barrier of some kind. Then the
hero sings to placate the power of place."

Some Navajo storytellers say that the most important
healing feature in the Featherway occurs in Part Four. This
is the visit of Sun Father's son to his parent's house. Psy-
chologically, entering the House of the Sun could not be a
more potent medicine for the patient suffering from lack of
sight. Spiritually, the son's reward for facing the hardships
of the journey culminates in the fight for his own identity.

For when he meets the Sun, he is almost denied seeing Him because of the Sun's jealous wife. He must then fight his father, proving that he is worthy to be the Sun's son. This would seem to be the final rite of passage expressed by the Featherway. Using a breath feather, the Sun's son demonstrates his worth by deflecting his father's arrows of lightning. It is after this trial that he is permitted to see the bountiful treasure of game animals that are prepared for The People in time to come. And it is through this ceremonial visit, in which a mortal is joined to an immortal, that the future blessing is assured.

Readers may note a similarity between First Boy's wife's unfaithfulness and Girl Who Walks Softly. Their predicament and the subsequent outcome are the same; this is because all Navajo origin stories borrow elements from each other. Perhaps they may be best described as a river of origin with many tributaries. Anthropologists have divided, characterized, and catalogued the main river—let us say, for argument's sake, it is the Blessingway—and subheaded the lesser Ways, those that came later, those that share only a small part of the whole; the Beadway, for instance, which Jay de Groat recently told me was "borrowed" or "influenced by" the Plains tribes. The Blessingway, emphasizing as it does tribal unity, sharing, harmony of family and clan, may have its own origin in religious practices learned by the Navajos from their historical predecessors in the Southwest, the Pueblos.

A Navajo storyteller, apart from a medicine man, would probably not call our Ways Ways at all, but might refer to them merely as winter stories, seasonal tales of the origin of The People. An anthropologist, however, might say there are only two basic Ways: Holyway and Blessingway, from which all the others flow as tributaries.

In any event, I have heard Part One of the Featherway

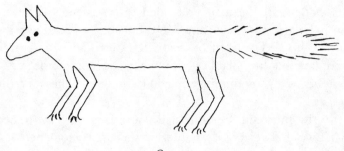

Coyote.

told as "The War Between Men and Women," with no reference to its being a Way at all. In the curative sense, all Ways lead to all other Ways because it is the whole body, the whole mind that is being healed by the whole prehistory of the tribe—"one vast interlocked myth," as Frank Waters called it.

PART ONE

In the Third World, there was no sun and the beings of that world lived in darkness.

Coyote lived in that world, and the one known as Shapeshifter, the one who could change into anything. They were spending a lot of time together, those two.

There was a woman. Her name was Girl Who Walks Softly. She was married to a man to whom she was unfaithful, and he did not know what to do about it. Every day, she would ask him to carry her down to the river.

"Husband," she said, "I need to cool my feet in the current."

So he took her down to the river and left her there. But when he went to carry her home, he saw that she was with two others—one who ran away and one who disappeared.

That night, the man pretended to be asleep. As he lay on his blanket he saw someone drop small sticks down the smoke hole. They fell on his wife's head, and she stirred and opened her blanket—for what, he could not see— but he felt something shift about in the stillness of the hogan.

In the morning, he grumbled, "Woman you have ruined what was between us. I know what you are doing when you think I am not looking."

The wife, knowing her husband's temper, kept quiet.

"I suppose I will just have to kill you," the husband said.

Then the woman got up and went out of the hogan. The man watched her, and again, it seemed that something not visible to him followed her down to the river.

The next day a man told the husband that he had seen his wife go down the river on a raft with two other men. "What did they look like?" the husband asked.

"One of them was furry, the other was shadowy," the man said.

"It is as I suspected," the husband said.

So The People decided that it was necessary to kill the woman who was unfaithful to her husband. But First Woman Chief would not let them do this.

"You will have to kill me first," she said with authority.

The People did not want to do this. First Woman Chief was very wise, so they asked her what they should do. "It is time," she said, "to part the men from the women. One on one side of the river; one on the other side."

The unfaithful wife lived with the women. But it seemed that the women suffered more than the men. They did not plant new crops. Instead, they used the ones that were already planted when the men were there with them. The women grew thin and weak, but the unfaithful wife was kept well because Coyote and Shapeshifter slipped across the river every day to feed her. The men witnessed this, and at last they decided to do something about it.

One day Coyote was caught stealing some of the men's food.

"You will die for this!" the man who caught him said. It was the husband whose wife had been unfaithful.

"If I die, you all will die," Coyote said.

Somehow, the men knew this was true, so they let him go.

And soon after this, other things happened that we know about: Coyote and Shapeshifter stole Water Monster's babies. Then, a strange light appeared in the east and Messenger Fly reported that a flood was coming.

The flood came, as we know, and The People escaped through the reed, and they climbed until they reached Hard Sky. When they got there, they tried to hold the water down, but they were not able to do it. The water kept rising. Now the Snake People worked hard to hold the water back—they worked so hard, that they hugged the water back until it froze off their arms and legs. This is why they have remained armless and legless since that time.

The water kept going up until Coyote was caught with Water Monster's babies. When he returned them, the water went down. Shapeshifter was the one who finally pushed it back where it belonged.

After the water went down, The People looked around. But they could not see very well because the only light in the world was a fog that hung over everything. It gave off a dark light.

At that time, First Woman Chief died and twin sons were born to Girl Who Walks Softly. In four days these sons turned into grown men (they became the Pollen Boys, but this comes later).

Now First Man and First Woman knew that The People wanted more light to see the new world. So they told The

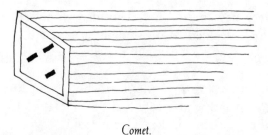

Comet.

People to put offerings on the wings of Bat. The People did this and the offerings turned into stars. But since the stars did not have life in them, First Man and First Woman told two boys to sing life into them. They began to do this when Coyote came along and stole the boys' voices. Therefore, the stars could not flicker the way they were supposed to.

The People gave Coyote offerings, and when he accepted them, he sang to the east, south, west, and north. Then light was breathed into the stars, and they began to shine. The constellations were next to go up into the sky. First Man and First Woman had worked out where they were going to put them. But Coyote got them and scattered them all over the place. This made more work for First Man and First Woman. They had to fix everything up again and blow on the sky until it was just the right height from the earth.

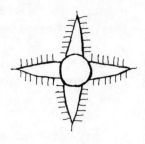

Star.

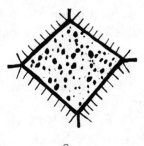

Star.

Coyote felt sorry for what he had done, and said: "I know you are mad at me because of the way I've behaved, but I will be the one to call for rain. And even if you do not like me, you will still need me for many things." Saying this, he went off on his way.

Now there was still much work to be done. The twin sons of Girl Who Walks Softly were given two baskets. In one basket was a turquoise, which was the sun; in the other basket was a white stone, which was the moon. The two Pollen Boys were told to carry these baskets separately, but Shapeshifter, who was the boys' father, objected.

He said, "I don't want my sons doing this!"

First Man and First Woman answered him: "It will be your duty to control all of the Animal People. Furthermore, it will be your special job to see your sons pass from east to west each day. Won't that please you?"

Shapeshifter did not answer right away. But everyone knew that he was content.

The Pollen Boys said, "Each day that we travel, as you say, from east to west, someone will die."

First Man and First Woman nodded that it was so.

Then Sun Pollen Boy spoke up: "There will be twelve paths for the sun. Some paths will have rain and some will not have rain."

He looked then at his brother, Moon Pollen Boy, and he said: "The moon will have no path, but will wander the heavens."

And it happened that Coyote did not like the new name given to him by First Man: First Angry. So he tried to steal the name of a mountain and then The People named him He Who Moves Everything That Grows. For a while, he was content.

Shapeshifter was given the honor of Guardian of the Animals, which later was changed to He Who Raises Deer.

Coyote started raising a fuss again; this time he wanted more duties. So First Man gave him control of wind, rain, and a part of childbirth, and for a while, he was content.

Changing Woman was born four years after this. The daughter of Earth and Sky, Changing Woman married the Sun and had two children: He Who Moves From The Right and He Who Moves From The Left. The first son became known as Monster Slayer; the second was called Born Of Water. After a time, so they say, Changing Woman went west to the Pacific Ocean and settled somewhere on an island. But there are those who say her sister did this, and that she has never gone anywhere, she is always here.

PART TWO

Time passed and the Sun had another boy who was born at a place near Zuni. When the boy was old enough to think of such things, he asked his mother who his father was, and his mother pointed to the Sun and said, "there." So the boy began to prepare for a long journey.

Spider Man gave the boy web to help him on his way, but he said, "You will never reach the Sun."

Spirit Wind helped the boy and took him to Fire God, who gave him a fire stick, but each of them said, "You will never reach the Sun."

Seed Bearers gave the boy breath feathers and the Arrow
People gave him arrow points, but they said to him, "You
will never reach the Sun."
The boy then began his hard journey.
He faced:

Cutting Knives
Strong Stream
Cutting Reeds
Craggy Cliff
Slippery Ice
Dangerous Dust
Wide River

The boy flew over cutting knives on his breath feathers.
He crossed strong stream on Frog's rainbow.
He burned cutting reeds with Spirit's wind
And Firegod's fire stick.
He crossed craggy cliff on Bat's back.
He crossed over slippery ice on Spider Man's web.
He crossed wide river on Water Spider's back.
And, at last, he reached the house of the Sun.

The boy stood before the doorway of his father's house.
There were four doorways leading into the house:

Door of Crooked Wind
Door of Great Snake
Door of Bear Guardian
Door of Lightning Guardian

The boy knew their names, and as he spoke them the
guardians opened the doors and the boy passed through.

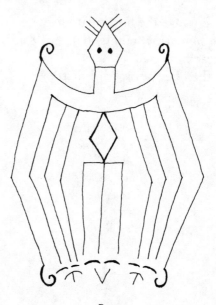

Bat.

Once inside he met the Sun's wife.
"Who are you?" she asked.
"I am the Sun's son," the boy said.
"Oh," she said in a jealous whisper.
Then she wrapped him in five whirlwinds:

> *Black of cloud*
> *White of sunrise*
> *Blue of noon*
> *Yellow of dusk*
> *Dark of night*

These were all very hot and he was burning in them, but then she unleashed icy rain and he froze. Then the Sun came in.
"Who is this?" he asked.
"Your son has come," she answered.

"Which son?"

"My mother told me I was yours," the boy said.

He was still imprisoned by the clouds and the rain. At a glance the Sun made them vanish. He looked at the boy, but the Sun was not convinced that it was his child.

"Here, my son," he said, and he fired a lightning bolt at the boy.

The boy raised the breath feathers and the lightning bolt went off in another direction.

"So, you are my son," the Sun smiled.

"Yes, Father."

The Sun called for his favorite daughter, Turquoise Girl. She came, and the boy met her. They liked each other.

Then the Sun said, "You may have a gift from my house."

The boy took a blanket with a sand painting of the Sun on it.

"It is a good choice," the Sun said.

Then the boy told the Sun what he had seen on earth. He told him how the Animal People had come into the world and how many good things there were, but that these good things had gone away, and now the earth was a place without goodness.

"Is that so?" the Sun said. He waved his arm and the doors of his house opened and out of the doors poured an endless flow of animals, who made a circle in the sky and returned into the house of the Sun.

The Sun said, "These things are not to be, just now. Tell your people to be patient. They will come to you, in time."

Then the Sun took the boy back down to earth and returned to the sky.

At the door of his mother's hogan, the boy appeared. His mother looked at him, and although he had not changed, she hardly recognized him. And he hardly recognized her, for she had grown so old in the time that he had been away.

Turkey.

"My son," she said, "is it really you?"

"Yes, mother," he answered. Then he told her of the doorways of the Sun and how they had opened and the animals that had flowed out of them.

"That is good," she said. "But you see how it is here. I am nearly starved for lack of food."

"You will not starve while I am around," he said.

And so the boy went on another long journey. He traveled on a raft with Turkey, who had grown very old, but also very wise. They went right past the Place Where The Rivers Cross. They came to a broad meadow. Here Turkey tied up the raft and shook out his wings. From Turkey's feathers fell a storm of seeds: corn, beans, tobacco, and squash.

"These will soon grow and nourish The People," Turkey said.

Their journey continued until they reached the hogan of the one who was once named Shapeshifter, but who was now called Guardian of the Game. By now he was an old

man, but he had a young daughter with whom the boy fell
in love. Soon they were married. The boy was given the
name, He Who Floats.

He Who Floats got to be a wise medicine man and he
went to live somewhere over by Zuni.

That is what they say, anyway.

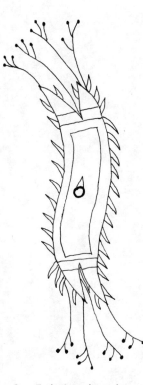

Sun Father's medicine bag.

THE
WATERWAY

Coyote as depicted by Navajo artist, Jay de Groat. As shown earlier, this
is a colored-paper design replicating a sand painting. Coyote is stealing
Water Monster's babies. From the top, Buffalo, Bat, and Bear look on.
From the bottom, Salamander, Otter, and Horned Toad look on.

I n the Waterway, Water Monster, the unruly one, is tamed
and made safe for The People. So, symbolically, is water
transformed and governed by The People for use in the

watering of plants in the desert. Water Monster, the mythological heart of water, must be appeased; the water ceremonies of this Way must be learned so that the forces of
rainfall will be cleansing and nourishing rather than destruc-
tive. Medicine men perform this rite on patients who have
had negative or damaging experiences with the power of
water: drowning, near drowning, even dreams of drowning.

The drama of Water Monster's taming in Part One is
followed in Part Two by the interaction of the Man of First
Earth and the people of the village. The villagers make the
mistake of shunning Man of First Earth's wives, who as a
result of their marriage to him, have become Bird People.
Their husband, through his travels and experiences, has
grown into a medicine man with bird and butterfly powers.
Noteworthy here is the fact that Navajos believe birds to be
emissaries of the Spirit World (regard Heron in Part Three)
and spiritual healers in their own right.

By turning their backs on his wives, the villagers also turn
on the Bird People. This is how they bring harmful rain
upon themselves. Lightning kills them, water rages and carries away their crops. In the end, the two villagers who
survive seek the obeisant action of prayers and offerings.
This releases the village from the dark spell that has been
hanging over it, and peace is again restored.

The storyteller of the Waterway uses a rich array of water
imagery in the myth. Lakes, springs, and rivers run through
the tale and, at the start of the story, a cottonwood tree is
depicted as an ally of the hero. The tree, which in the
Southwest thrives in and around water, is the symbolic shel-
ter and life-preserving craft upon which the hero is carried
through his adventure. By felling the tree and making a log
boat of it, the hero is protected by "crooked and straight
lightning."

There are many characters in the drama of the Waterway

but perhaps the most significant is Fire God. It is Fire God who overcomes Water Monster's smug condescension in the cave. Fire as metaphor may be seen as an extension of The People's growth from the prior worlds of darkness into the upper worlds of light. Through the use of fire, they become masters of their environment; water, in the story, is balanced by fire. Fire God, as a symbolic being, exemplifies the power of flame as a practical tool for The People to raise themselves out of a harsh environment.

However, it should be noted that fire, water, earth, and air are not just elements, but godlike presences in the Waterway. Consider, if you will, that there is a scientific, as well as mythic, progression of thinking in this and other origin stories. Our earth was formed out of the crucible of heat and light, water and oxygen—so, too, does the emergence theme of the Waterway deal with the dark incubation of life as it travels through the watery womb of the Mother into the sphere of the Sun Father's light.

All of the stories, but especially the Waterway, move through dark tunnels, or nightlit places, to fields of light. What Navajo storytellers are implicitly telling us in the Waterway is that to be whole, to be one with the universe, Man must return, metaphorically, to the Mother. Water and fecundity are intertwined in the Waterway which, in addition to being a curing rite, is a fertility myth: "Then Man of First Earth raised up a corn plant . . . and it rained gently for four days and the corn rose out of the mud, and grew."

PART ONE

There was a poor beggar man from Zuni who was known as Person Wishing for Something. He wore a deerskin over his shoulders and deer horns on his head for a mask while he

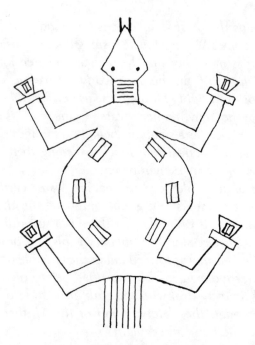

Water Monster.

was out hunting near his grandmother's house. One day he
ran into a coyote who tricked him. The coyote cast a spell
on the poor man, took the deer hide and mask, and ex-
changed it for his own coyote skin.

After four days, people went out looking for the man.
They found an old coyote under a bush. The only thing the
man could utter were coyote noises, so the people took him
back to the village, built some hoops, and did the changing-
back ceremony to make him a man again. Then the poor
beggar man found the coyote and switched skins with him.

Then the man left his village and journeyed over to Hopi
country. He was not well-received there because he was a
wanderer. So he returned home and got his grandmother,

and together they went to Kaibitoh Spring. The Hopis pur-
sued them, but Spirit Wind helped them escape on a rainbow four times.

After this, they went to the place where the old ones lived
long ago. The old ones were called Ahnah Suzzie. They left
this place and went to Round Lake. From there they went
north to the La Plata Mountains. It was there the man began
to make a boat beside the La Plata River.

Talking God came up to him one day and said: "What are
you doing?"

"Trying to make a boat," the man said. He was tying some
reeds together to fashion a raft, but it was of poor quality.

Talking God went to talk it over with the Holy People.
Elder Brother and Younger Brother offered to help, and so
did the other deities. Then Elder Brother and Younger
Brother gave a great shout and the cottonwood tree by the
river shook by the roots and toppled over on its side. The
Wind People came and hollowed the tree out. They put
White Cloud at the stern and prow and decorated the boat
with Rainbow. Then they carved four rock crystal windows
in the sides of the boat, and it was ready for the man to use.

The deities came to seem him off. Cyclone and Big Hail
went with him, Crooked and Straight Lightning protected
him. On the banks of the river the man's pet turkey followed
him as he journeyed out into the swift current. In three days,
the man floated to the place where Water Monster lived.
There, the man and the boat disappeared. When he did not
show up at the Place of Falling Water, Talking God went
looking for him.

He found him in Water Monster's Cave.

"Will you let my grandson free?" Talking God asked.

In the corner of the cave, he saw the poor man huddled,
covered with green slime.

Water Monster answered, "Why should I help you?"

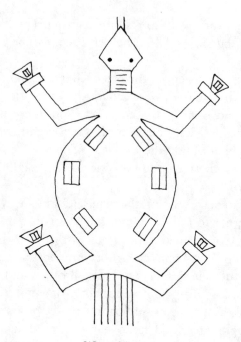

Water Monster.

So Talking God sought Fire God. "Water Monster is holding our grandson prisoner," he said.

Fire God accepted the challenge and together they went
back to Water Monster's cave. The poor man had more
slime hanging off him.

"It is time to let our grandson go," Fire God announced.

Water Monster said, "What for?"

"Release him at once or I will punish you severely," Fire
God replied.

Water Monster shrugged his blue and white shoulders,
and green slime came off them and fell in a pool on the floor
of the cave.

"I do not have to answer you," he said.

Then Fire God set fire to the water all around the cave. The water crackled with bluish green flame. Water Monster backed away, shivering. He had never seen anything like it. "You may take the man," he said, "and go away from here." Fire God then put out the watery fire, and the man continued on his journey. But as soon as he left the cave, his boat bogged in slime, and he himself was so covered with it that he became paralyzed.

A ceremony was prepared by the Holy People. It was called the Bathing Ceremony.

First they cleansed him of Water Monster's slime, but the man still could not speak and his eyes were frozen open. Frog and Turtle came and performed their ceremony over the man. Now his eyes would work, but he still could not speak. Otter and Beaver came and performed their ceremony over the man, but he still could not speak. So Two Thunder People came and they gave the man the Bathing Ceremony once again, and this time it worked and the man was cured. Then the man camped in the place that was flat by the river, and Turkey was with him. The Holy People spread a robe for Turkey to stand on and they told him to shake out his wings.

Turkey shook out:

> *White corn*
> *Yellow corn*
> *Blue corn*
> *Many-colored corn*

And the other seeds of life fell out of Turkey's feathers, and in four days the corn was grown and in four more it was ripe. So the man told Turkey he had done his work well, and he should now live in the mountain where all turkeys live today.

Round Lake.

PART TWO

The man then went back up the river where he sang four songs the Holy People taught him. He then went back to see his grandmother, and she asked about his journey, but he did not tell her anything.

In time he became a good bird-snarer, using his own hair to make snares for sparrows. He wetted himself in Round Lake and rolled himself in feathers to get warm. He became a feather-changer and the people made fun of him.

Then the man dressed himself in woodpecker feathers, nuthatch feathers, mountain tanager feathers, sparrow feathers, bluebird feathers, and feathers of the rock wren. And he went to Aztec to marry two girls who lived there. They were doing embroidery when he met them.

One of the girls said: "How pretty that bird is there."

Quickly, he changed into a black and yellow butterfly, then a black and white butterfly, then a yellow and red butterfly, then he sprinkled pollen on the girls and he turned into a red butterfly. They followed him out into the bright sunlight and saw him land on a corn plant.

"Come home with me," the man said in the voice of Corn bug, so the girls followed him home, but the moment he got there, he rolled in feathers and turned into a bird, and the

Bird People.

girls rolled in the feathers and they too turned into Bird People.

In time the girls grew restless and the man told them they should go back to their village. They agreed and he gave them a bulrush and a breath feather to protect them on their way.

In the village the people were angry with the two girls. One wore turquoise in her hair and the other wore white shell. The villagers thought the girls looked and smelled different and they whipped them with willow wands. So one girl threw down the bulrush and a cloud of pollen covered the two of them. The other girl threw down the breath feather and a black cloud took them away from the village.

When the girls got back to their husband, they told him what had happened. He did not say anything.

"Please," they begged, "you must punish our people for being so rude—"

But he refused.

They said, "We have thirty-two brothers who should all be punished!"

Then the man made an arrow and a basket. He shot the arrow and it rained hard on the girls' village. Then he threw down the basket and it rained harder. Then the river rose and the corn and squash and beans got washed away, and the people were washed away with them. The only people left were the mother and father of the two girls. And the man took a look at what he had done to the village. He walked around in the rain and looked at everything. The father and mother of the girls saw him there.

"You are a Man of First Earth," they said.

He nodded that it was so.

"Can you not make peace and plenty come again?" they asked. They gave him fine silver jewelry and other good offerings.

He nodded, "I can make things go back the way they were," he said. Then he walked over four people who had been killed by lightning, and, as he stepped over them, the people came to life.

"Can you make the crops come back?" the mother asked.

"You must go away now," he told her, "do not look at what I do."

She and her husband obeyed.

Then the Man of First Earth raised up a corn plant in three secret places. And he raised one up at each of the four quarters of the field and in the middle, and it rained gently for four days and the corn rose out of the mud, and grew.

And grew.

And life was restored to the village.

PART THREE

The Man Of First Earth then took his wives with him; they followed Heron into the sky. They went all the way to the

Sun. As they passed him, he looked back at them, twice.
The Man Of First Earth met Lightning, and Lightning
gave him a new name: Thunder Boy. When they came to
the top of the sky, they crossed:

> Black Peak Rocks
> Straight Lightning Path
> Crystal Path
> Rainbow Path

They were at the edge of the sky where Spider makes his
hole-house. They watched Spider blow twice into the hole
and it got big enough for them to enter.

"Ho," Spider chuckled as they came into his hole-house,
"White Butterfly stole the two girls—"

And he laughed out loud, and you can hear his laughter
now, if you listen.

THE
WINDWAY

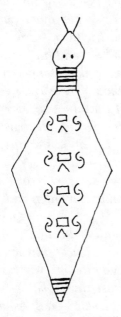

Great Snake symbol with deer-tracks on his back; also note forked tongue and tail rattle.

Tony Hillerman tells the story of the Valencia County man who asks his Navajo friend to build some fences for him over by Redondo Mesa. When the Navajo is warned about the snakes that live out there, he shrugs it off, saying: "Snakes are friends of the Navajo." The next day when the landowner hauls some wire out to the fence site, he sees dead snakes lying all over the lava rocks. "How come you told me rattlesnakes and Navajos are friends?" the man asks. The Navajo replies that there were so many "friends," he couldn't get any wire strung.

This is a contemporary story, presumably true. I have told it to Navajos who think it is funny, but from the perspective of "the old ways," the Navajo who killed so many snakes would find himself in psychic, moral, and physical distress. Once I told a Navajo friend how my brother had killed a rattlesnake to make a belt, and how, having cut the snake's head partially off, the snake whipped around and bit him. My brother almost died. The Navajo who heard the story did not smile when I told the conclusion: "My brother has not killed another snake." He felt that the killing of a rattlesnake to decorate a belt was vanity, and as such, was punished by "the law of nature."

In the Windway we see power of Great Snake and his relationship to Lightning, Thunder, and Wind. Medicinally, the myth and chant of the Windway help to cure "snake infection," which includes a host of illnesses. Some of these are heart and lung problems, stomach trouble, infection, body itching, and eye trouble. Mythologically, however, the chant warns against the violation—as in my brother's case—of the ancient Navajo codes. As cited in the tale that follows, these include the eating of an already dead, not freshly killed, animal; eating the intestines of that animal; and ignoring the dominion of Great Snake.

The connection between Great Snake and his representatives on earth, that is, all snakes, should be noted, as well as the tie between Great Snake, Thunder, and Lightning. Great Snake's retributive power derives from being able to call forth Thunder and Lightning. Symbolically, Snake, Lightning, and Arrow are closely related. In sand paintings, the two-headed arrow looks like lightning. Snakes, which are often designed as zigzags, or lightninglike motifs, are sometimes shown with lightning coming out of their mouths.

Navajo mythology often depicts the snake as a link between the worlds of Earth and Sky. The Feathered Serpent, part bird, part snake, is perhaps one of the oldest archetypes of this ancient union. It is interesting to note here, in the same context, that in Navajo sand paintings the marking on Snake's back is the symbol for brotherhood, again emphasizing the positive link between the worlds of earth and sky, man and reptile.

Navajo mythology shows the positive power of Snake, Thunder, Lightning, and Wind. But it also shows how, when human transgression is present, these forces work against human will, and become detrimental. Navajos say that Wind comes in many forms: mild, intoxicating, wild, unruly. Thus, Wind can be good or bad, and like Snake, can hide almost anywhere. Invisible, Wind can enter a man's inner ear, and influence his innermost thoughts. Little Wind, therefore, is the informer, Big Wind the warrior.

In the Windway, Elder Brother discovers that only through propitiation can he shed the skin of the snake. As in most of the other Ways, he must pass through the ceremonial hoops to gain back his human form. Working with Wind, Elder Brother's family must learn not to be afraid of Great Snake. Fear, it is seen in the tale, must be overcome. Paralyzed, Elder Brother learns what happens when a man violates the codes previously cited. "Great Snake," he confides at the end, "punished me terribly."

It is up to the Wind People to save him. They must blow the life-breath into his fingers to bring him back to normal. And again, Elder Brother learns that fear, in and of itself, is a kind of disease. "You must remember not to fear the Wind People," he remarks to Younger Brother, "because we Earth People are a part of them." The ultimate message of the Windway is just that—Snake, Wind, Thunder, and Lightning are part of the pattern of life that must be followed in order to live in harmony. In the cave of Great Snake the

*lesson is learned: Be humble, obey the code, show no fear.
If one does not forget these things, all will be well. But if one
does forget, there is always the Windway.*

PART ONE

There was a man of the Deer Clan who had a wife, two sons,
and a daughter. He lived on a mountain north of Taos. One
afternoon the elder brother saw a large deer track, which he
followed until it grew dark. Then he went home and told his
family what he had seen.

The next morning he went out again, staying on the
deer's trail until he reached Red Mountain, near Cabezon
Peak. To his surprise, the deer he had been tracking was
dead. He wondered about this, how it had happened, but it
did not stop him from butchering the meat. Later on, he
cooked the deer's intestines and began to eat them. While
he was swallowing, the intestines turned into a snake. At the
same time, he turned into one himself, a blue racer. Afterward, he crawled off into the cave of Great Snake.

That night, when their boy did not return, the family sat
up waiting for him. At dawn Talking God appeared at the
doorway of their hogan and told them what had happened.
So the father went out in search of his son.

When he got to Red Mountain, approaching from the
east just as his son had done, Blue Racer suddenly rushed at
him, hissing angrily. Even though he knew the snake was his
son, he was still frightened of it.

In the morning Cousin Fly told the father that he must
journey toward Mt. Taylor to see the Wind People. They
were an old couple, a man and woman with wild, windy
hair. All around their hogan were red-painted dancers who
danced and waved their arms.

The father made an offering of buckskin to the old couple, but they would not accept it, so he made another, this time placing turquoise, jet, white shell, and abalone—four stones for the four directions—on the buckskin. This time the old couple accepted them. The old man said, "There will be a ceremony to get your son back. I will send out Wind Messengers to spread the word."

The father went home, satisfied. The next morning he and his family returned to Red Mountain where the ceremony was going to be held. The Wind People had made four hoops: black, blue, yellow, and one of many colors. The hoops were bound with yucca-string and pine twigs, and placed in a line to the east of Great Snake's cave. The Wind People and Thunder People were dressed in their finest flint.

"Give this offering," Old Man Wind said to the father. "Offer it to Great Snake, and make sure, when you give it to him, that you do not show your fear."

The father went into the cave, and lightning flashed.

Once inside, he looked down at his feet. He stood, ankle-deep, in a nest of angry snakes. The father, though he was frightened, did not show his fear.

Out of the mass of snakes, he saw Blue Racer, his son. He reached out and grabbed his son and took him outside, writhing and striking, into the sunlight.

Then the Wind People took Blue Racer and passed him through the hoops. As he went through the hoops, Blue Racer cracked open. The elder brother's human head came through the mouth of the blue racer snake. Then, just as a snake sheds its skin, the boy came out of the blue racer's body.

But though he was human again, the elder brother could not move because he was still paralyzed. He said, "Great Snake punished me terribly."

Wind and Thunder saw that it was so. And the Wind People gave him another curing ceremony, blowing life-breath into his fingers and toes and body parts. With a roaring stick, they drove off the bad spirits. With holy plant bundles and healing songs, they sang the elder brother back to health. For four days and four nights they sang over him. But at the end of that time, he was not well.

Then Blue Wind bathed him and pressed a snake-painted cloth to the boy's hands, but he only got well for a short time. After that, he got weak and grew blind. Now, Blue Wind made a cloth which had Wind People, Thunder People, Snake People, and Star People on it, and this was just like a sand painting. But the boy would not come out of the sickness.

Finally, a fourth ceremony was held in front of the cave of Great Snake. Yellow Wind called the medicine man from the top of the San Francisco Peaks. He made a sun painting and the elder brother was told to lie down upon it. Monster Slayer and Born of Water and Changing Woman came and brought a crystal bowl with them to bless the ceremony.

The elder brother was bathed: He had a sun painted on his chest and a wind person was riding over the sun. A moon was painted on his back, lines led down his arms ending in arrow points. Snakes went down both his legs, and on his shoulders he wore a white cross and on his forehead a prayer plume. White on his forehead, and red across his eyes with yellow across the chin, completed him.

Then the elder brother was fed cornmeal by Bluejay and Whirling Wind.

And the ceremony was finished.

PART TWO

When he was himself again, the elder brother taught his younger brother the ceremony which the Holy People had taught him. "You must remember not to fear the Wind

People," he said, "for we Earth People are a part of them. All that I have been taught, and tell you now—I must return to the Wind."

So saying, he embraced his family for the last time. Then the Wind People took him away with them and he was never seen again on earth. But his spirit is always there, on the wind's breath.

THE
EVIL-CHASING
WAY

The story is told of a Navajo man who was attending an Evil-Chasing Way near his home in Crownpoint, New Mexico. He was standing under the juniper arbor, the place where meals are prepared after the ceremony, when he noticed a bullet that had been fired into one of the wooden posts. Lodged in the cedar, the bullet offered proof that there was something out of harmony in his life. Since no shot had been fired, and the bullet looked fresh in the splintered wood, the man felt that this was a warning.

As the man explained it later on: "Sheep were killed for the feast after the Way, and instead of destroying the hides of the sheep by burning them, I sold them to a dealer in town. At the dealer's shop, I saw that one of the hides had been marked with four lines; one line for each month that would pass before an unexplainable event would come."

Four months passed. In November, twenty of the man's sheep were slaughtered by a skinwalker, a Navajo sorcerer. "Then more and more bad things started to happen," he explained. "I was cleaning my gun when it accidentally fired, nearly killing my sister. Then I took sick and almost died."

Did the Evil-Chasing Way help to protect the man and his family from witchcraft?

"It saved us," he replied. "It blessed and protected, and the well-being of our family was kept, even though the witch stalked the ranch at night."

Anthropologists have said that the Evil-Chasing Way has its origin in stories of the Slaying of Monsters. Following The People's emergence into the fourth world, Monster Slayer destroyed the mythic monsters of Navajoland, which left a residue of evil on the land. This residual darkness, so to speak, sapped the earth of its vitality. The Evil-Chasing Way was created to compensate the earth for this offense, and to protect human beings from the monster's malignity (even in death). Essentially, the Evil-Chasing Way is a ceremonial created to destroy the power of ghosts, evil-doers who use ghost power in witchcraft, or any negative association with either of these.

The myth of the Evil-Chasing Way is similar to the Windway, yet the focus of the story is sharper, the characters better delineated. The homage which one must pay for harmony is shown dramatically in this tale. The lesson spoken by Elder Brother has to do with illness and suffering: "Learn to protect yourselves," he warns, "against the powers of illness." Here, he points out, illness itself may be thought of as a malign force, for he refers to it as "the powers of illness."

He adds that one must not "watch anything suffering or dying." I have heard Navajos express this same opinion, but they have added, by way of explanation, "that you must not watch, with interest, the suffering of others." In other words, there are times in one's life when it is not possible to avoid seeing suffering. What a person must not do is watch it, on purpose, or because he wants to. If such a thing should happen, the Evil-Chasing Way is there to protect you from your "bad self."

In a positive way, the Evil-Chasing Way draws the human mind into its proper place of meditation, thus breaking the spell of suffering. As preventive medicine, The Evil-Chasing Way works against any kind of "stalking evil," but it also cures paralysis, deafness, swollen limbs, and such specific Navajo illnesses as "ghost sickness," dreams of ghosts and evil spirits, venereal disease, and other "night-related fears."

The characters here are the deities who control the forces of chaos. Talking God, Fire God, Water God, Earth Boy,

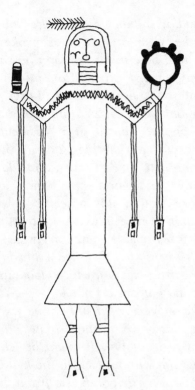

Fire God carrying fire stick and traveler's bread.

Wind, and Great Snake are all part of the pantheon of power. When the dark forces rule, these deities are out of harmony and must be appeased in the proper way.

The myth of the Evil-Chasing Way shows the difference in the personalities of Elder Brother and Younger Brother, who are references to Monster Slayer and Born of Water. In Part One, the bold, adventuresome Elder Brother ignores his brother's caution about not killing and eating a snake. Elder Brother kills it, eats it, and is subsequently turned into one. Part Two involves the help offered by Earth Boy to free Elder Brother of Great Snake's spell. Through the advice

given by Earth Boy and the power of Fire God, Elder Brother
is freed from the evil spirit. Part Three invokes Great Snake's
magic chant, told here in poetry form because of its ceremonial imagery. Elder Brother is told by Great Snake: "Do
not eat the intestines, heart, or liver of deer, nor kill or eat
woodrats or rabbits, nor eat anything that died naturally or
was killed by another animal, or by accidental means, and
you must not ever watch anything suffering or dying . . . this
last is most important." In Part Four, again, Elder Brother errs
by killing and eating a woodrat, and once again, Earth Boy
and other deities restore him to health.

It is interesting to note in this myth that the taboos presented are also reasonable "outdoor advice." For instance,
eating meat that is not freshly killed is a bad idea, and there
are poisons in certain cacti for which woodrats seem to have
an immunity that humans do not.

Great Snake, especially, should not be taken lightly. We
have witnessed his power in the Windway, but we did not
see the extent of it, or how it might be "charmed," other
than by facing him without fear. In the Evil-Chasing Way,
Great Snake's power is that of the earth and the underworld,
which is just below our present plane of existence. Perhaps,
as representative of the subconscious of man, Great Snake
must be dealt with in his own dark lair.

Great Snake in this myth represents an earth power that
must be mediated. Elder Brother does not read the "deer-
track marks" on the snake's back correctly, for they are a
warning. For the same token, the man stalked by the skinwalker did not read the four lines on the sheep hides with
clear judgment.

Navajos believe in the Biblical premise that pride goes
before the fall, that vanity is man's downfall. Elder Brother's
lapse of humility costs him plenty. The price is paid in
suffering. During such times, when caution is ignored, the

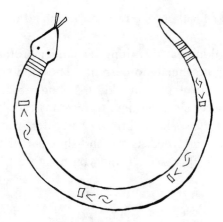

Curved Serpent Guard.

dark forces come into play. The Evil-Chasing Way is a way to bow before the unseen, and put a shield around oneself and one's family.

In the Evil-Chasing Way, Elder Brother is the first healer to learn the ways of hand-trembling from Gila Monster. What he learns becomes, as the Navajos put it, "that which he knows," a body of intuitive lore that cannot be expressed in words.

PART ONE

One time Elder Brother and Younger Brother were hunting around the mesa where Great Snake lived. Now, at this time, they did not know who, or what, Great Snake was.

Elder Brother saw a creature coiled under a bush. It had deer-track marks on its back. Elder Brother wanted to kill and eat the creature, but Younger Brother did not think this was a good idea. After hesitating to kill it three times, on the fourth, Elder Brother killed the creature and cooked it over a fire.

"We shouldn't eat this thing," Younger Brother said.

But Elder Brother ignored him. "There's no harm in it."

The next morning, at first light, Younger Brother did not find his brother sleeping next to him. Instead, lying beside the bones of the snake his brother had eaten, he saw another snake. This one rattled its tail and shot out its tongue.

Younger Brother said, "I told you not to eat it."

PART TWO

Now, there was a youth, the nephew of Elder Brother, who lived nearby. He happened also to be the grandson of Great Snake. He knew what had happened to Elder Brother because Messenger Wind had breathed the story into his ear. So he told Younger Brother about the mountain to the south that was shaped like a coiled snake.

Then Younger Brother and his family journeyed to that mountain. They went with Talking God, who told them when they got there that he alone would enter Great Snake's cave.

Once inside the cave, he spoke: "I come after my grandson."

In the half-light of the cave he saw two Snake People: Great Snake Man and Great Snake Woman. They were at rest, lying in the darkness.

Great Snake Man spoke back: "No creature that walks on earth should ever enter our den. Be gone!"

Talking God left without saying more.

Time went by, and Talking God and Elder Brother's family tried to gain entrance to the cave, but always they were turned away with hissing noises.

Then Messenger Fly came to them and said, "The only one who can help you is Earth Boy, the one who is the nephew of Elder Brother."

"Now, nephew," Younger Brother said, "I know your true name and will call you by it. You are called Nourished by the Growth of the Earth. Can you bring back Elder Brother?"

"Since you have called my true name, I will do what you ask," he replied.

Then, his name's power having been used, Earth Boy was now able to help his family. He said, "At the place called Wooded Hill there are five elders: four Fire Gods and one Water God."

Younger Brother asked, "What can they do?"

"They can bring Elder Brother back."

It happened that Fire God went into Great Snake's cave with his fire stick and Water God went in with him with his water jar.

"Is our grandson here?" they asked. They repeated the question four times.

Each time, Great Snake writhed about angrily and hissed a warning that they should leave. His tail quivered and made the sound of rattling pebbles.

"Will you not give us your help?" Fire God asked.

"That is right!" Great Snake hissed.

So he asked three more times, and each time he spoke, Great Snake's tail buzzed loudly and his eyes burned brightly, and a wind came up in the cave and wrestled around on the floor. Then Fire God raised his fire stick and spun it on the floor of the cave with his foot. Smoke rose up all around them.

"Ha!" Great Snake laughed scornfully. "Is that all you can do?"

Fire God spun the fire stick more vigorously and more smoke filled the cave, but Great Snake spat at it, paid no attention. Then he spun the fire stick so fast that flames leaped off it and filled the cave. Great Snake only warmed his cold skin against the heat.

"Ha!" he hissed, "That is nothing!"

Fire God then spun the fire stick so that it caused the cave walls to tremble. Then the whirling stick rose up and shot a fireball into Great Snake's face. This made him draw back in fear, as the whole cave filled with firelight and smoke.

"You may have your grandson now," he said, in defeat.

The moment he said this, Water God put out the fire.

"Your grandson is up there," Great Snake said, thrusting his head at the rafters.

Up above, wrapped around a beam, they saw him for the first time: Elder Brother who had been changed into a snake.

"You cannot have him yet," Great Snake hissed.

"What must we do?" Fire God asked.

Great Snake said, "You must give me what is due."

"And what might that be?"

"A diamond-shaped shell."

"Is that all you require?"

"There is one more thing," Great Snake said, "You must learn my ceremonial song, the Evil-Chasing Chant."

"It is agreed," Fire God said.

PART THREE

Great Snake made a black mountain facing east
He made a blue mountain pointing east
He made a yellow mountain, white mountain
He made a rose hoop, a yellow, a blue, and a black rose hoop
He picked up Elder Brother, still a snake, passed him
    by the south sides of the hoops and mountains

He stood, then, at the east end of the path
He prayed before the white mountain with two white bear tracks
He prayed the dangerous powers to go away
He prayed on blue bear mountain bear tracks
He prayed on yellow bear mountain bear tracks
He prayed on black bear mountain bear tracks
He sang, he prayed, he stepped over the mountain
He sang and he prayed and he threw Elder Brother who was still a snake
    into the hoop of rose
And Elder Brother became a man once more.

Then he spoke to all who were gathered:
"This you shall learn to protect yourselves against the powers of illness. I will now teach you the ceremony of chasing away dangerous powers. Remember: Do not eat the intestines, heart, or liver of deer, nor kill or eat woodrats or rabbits, nor eat anything that died naturally or was killed by another animal, or by accidental means, and you must not ever watch anything suffering or dying . . . this last is most important."

But although Elder Brother was now a man, he was still paralyzed and deaf. Great Snake told his family to take him back to Coiled Mountain. There, at the same place where he killed the snake, he gathered bitter plants, sweet plants and berries, and from a lightning-struck tree he got bark and mixed all of these into a drink and drank it and poured and rubbed the rest over his body.

Then he vomited up the rest of the snake. And he was well.

PART FOUR

Sometime after this, Elder Brother and Younger Brother were again on a hunt. Elder Brother discovered a wood rat, and he killed it.

"We must not eat of that," Younger Brother warned, "it is forbidden."

Elder Brother skinned the animal, saying, "This is for our mother."

After he said it, he was hit on the ankle with sharp little needles.

"Hey," he called to Younger Brother, "Don't do that!"

Younger Brother was far away from him by that time, and he called out: "I'm not doing anything—what are you talking about?"

A little while later, Elder Brother's ankle was so swollen he could not walk on it. Younger Brother told him to sit quiet while he went and got Earth Boy.

When Earth Boy saw the little holes in Elder Brother's skin, he said to him: "You've stumbled into a cactus."

"I haven't," Elder Brother groaned.

"Then what are these holes doing here?"

"I don't know—"

"Then I'll tell you what I have heard," Earth Boy said. "I heard that Yellow Wind is punishing you for killing one of those small animals. You know, Woodrat eats cactus. That is why Yellow Wind threw cactus needles at your foot."

"—What can I do now?" Elder Brother asked.

They went to the home of Yellow Wind, and made a small shell basket offering. Yellow Wind took it and said he would come the following day. This, he did, bringing with him his medicine pouch. He took out a pinch of herbs, and put it on the swollen ankle and then he put a buckskin on him and pointed him north:

> Four zigzag lines of lightning in the dust
> East
> Four zigzag lines of lightning in the dust
> South

West
North

Then he crossed each one with a straight line and rubbed each one out with a prayer. Starting north, he made four lines at Elder brother's head, rubbed them and made them and rubbed them west, south, east, lifted the buckskin and . . .

And Elder Brother was well once more.

Then Yellow Wind took Elder Brother to the place where Gila Monster Guardians watch over:

> *Black Guardian to the east*
> *Blue Guardian to the south*
> *Yellow Guardian to the west*
> *White Guardian to the north*

For it is the power of Gila Monster to heal and the shaking hand of Elder Brother was a sign that the power of the lizard was now within him. Soon after, he began to have visions and Yellow Wind told him one thing more: "You must remember to tell The People not to lie in those places where wind sweeps across the Plain, that is my wish."

And his wish was done.

THE
MOUNTAINTOP
WAY

In the Mountaintop Way the storyteller speaks of the power of bears. This is not a transformation story like the Moving Up Way where Bear Woman attacks and kills her brothers. Rather, the Mountaintop Way shows the true spirit of bears: moody, sometimes vengeful creatures, who are also considered to be healers. As a ceremony, the Mountaintop Way may invoke rain and good crops; it may relieve coughing spells (which bears are thought to give); it may also relieve bad dreams about bears, and even bad luck brought about by thoughts of them. In addition, it is considered an excellent Way for starting a trip and ensuring safety.

In Navajo country, when the Mountaintop Way is done as a healing ceremony, it must be performed in the wintertime when bears hibernate. The belief is that the spirit of the bear might be offended during the warmer months when bears are moving around. In the myth itself there is the sense that the hero and heroine may, at any time, be made prisoner or be harmed by a bear attack. Yet the moral of the tale is that by confronting the bear, living with it, being born into its mythic world, the Mountaintop Way weaves the supernatural bears into the psyche of human beings. By the end of the tale—having felt the crush as well as the embrace of the spirit bear—the listener is made strong, the patient is made well.

How did bears get to be responsible for so many mixed blessings? Partly it is their nature, as viewed by the Navajo, and partly it is the presence of good and bad bears in myths that have made them what they are to The People. The story of the Mountaintop Way follows the progress of a Navajo war party to Taos Pueblo. There, two Pueblo girls

are taken prisoner. Our story really begins after their capture and release. For it is after they are free that they go on
a mystic journey. The older girl's journey, which deals with
the enchantment of bears, is the story of the Mountaintop
Way.

In the Mountaintop Way we learn that the bear is a divine
animal who possesses good and bad qualities. In order to
bring these into balance, the bear must be understood and
pacified. Only then can its potent medicine be used. The
dual role of the bear can be seen in many other Ways, as
well as this one. In the Featherway, the bear is the guardian
of the Sun Father's house, while in the Moving Up Way it
is the rampant Changing Bear Woman who kills her brother.
An animal of both madness and motherliness, the bear is
mysterious, looming, and melodramatic, inspiring a wide
range of human emotions.

Some of the things that bears do naturally have been

Bear Constellation symbol. Note that Bear was a guardian of Changing
Woman when she went on her travels; Bear is thus, in this instance, a sky
protector.

woven into Navajo mythology. For instance, when walking about in the forest, bears often cough or make huffing sounds—this was why The People believed they caused coughing sickness. The temper of the bear is like a raging storm. Navajos respect the bear's anger, but they also fear it, believing it can bring on madness. Bears are also fond of roaming and their territory is sometimes quite large. In the Mountaintop Way a lot of ground is covered, and when Changing Woman went on a long journey in an earlier part of this myth (not recorded here), she took along a bear as a bodyguard. These familiar attributes of the bear are not confined to legend, but are just like the ones we recognize in bears we see today.

The Mountaintop Way invokes unseen—and even un-known—mystical powers within the mysterious province of the bear and also the owl. The story of Owl Boy is told in Part Five of the Mountaintop Way, and it shows the nega-tive role of the owl in Navajo myths. The owl is a fearful bird whose nocturnal habits are frightening to traditional Navajos. With the watchful and protective presence of the Sun Father gone during the night hours, anything can hap-pen. As shown in the story, Owl Boy is not meant to live with The People because he is too unpredictable and dan-gerous. To this day, in most Native American tribes, owls are the callers of death, the singers of bad omens.

In Part One of the Mountaintop Way we learn how Bear and Snake captivate two young pueblo girls. The elder girl sleeps with Bear, and thus becomes the first of The People to give birth to a bear-child. Part Two comprises her mythic journey all around Navajoland, but particularly in "the home of the bears." The meaning of the Mountaintop Way, in Navajo, is literally "a chant toward a place within the moun-tains," and the bear in Navajo mythology is a creature "truly reared within the mountains." In Part Three, elder sister, who is now known as "Bear Woman," has a son who carries

forth the traveling theme of this myth. Eventually, in Part
Four, we find that Bear Woman's son gives birth to a child
who is an owl, and a whole new journey begins. Part Five
concludes with Owl Boy's elder brother and his own adventuresome life as an escapee from the Navajo's traditional
enemy, the Utes.

The Mountaintop Way has a secondary theme, which
deals with the helping roles of many of the "animal people"
who live among the mountains. The elder brother of Part
Five becomes acquainted with a whole host of secret animal
presences—unknown to the Utes in the story—who save
his life. In Part One, elder sister is saved by "a chipmunk
who took pity on her and brought her to a cave." In Part
Two, Deer People, Mountain Sheep People, Mountain Jay
People, Squirrel People, and others show their willingness
to serve as physical helpers and spiritual allies. It is in Part
Two that we discover that "Bear Sister's true name was Sickness." And so it is believed by many Navajos that the main
curing rite of this ceremonial is a "power over bears," or
overcoming the bear's inherent inclination to do harm and
cause trouble. But perhaps even greater than this motif is the
traveler's tale. For, just as Bear was once Mother Earth's
traveling companion, so should he be the guardian of man.
Long ago a young Navajo's rite of passage was to chase a
bear, or secretly stalk it, just to be able to touch it. If the
bear, in wheeling about and chasing the boy, failed to harm
or maim him, he was said to have "bear power."

PART ONE

There was a family that lived near Horse Lake, in Apache
country. The brothers of that family went about killing the
cliff dwellers who lived nearby.

One day, the brothers—there were twelve in all—found the cave dwellers holding an eagle ceremony. They killed all of the eagle dancers, but the other cave dwellers came after them and cornered them on the edge of a cliff.

They were in a desperate situation, so the brothers cut up some piñon trees and put prayer feathers in them. Then they hid the younger brother in the tree, and pitched it over the cliff. The younger brother landed safely—they heard his owl cry afterward. They cut another tree and hid the next older brother in it. That one got away safely too—they heard his coyote cry when he landed.

Suddenly, the cave dwellers made an attack on the remaining brothers and managed to kill all of them. But the two youngest made off in the darkness. Later, when they got back to Horse Lake, they called a council. Talking God, who had yellow hair and grey eyes, showed up. He told them to go back to the cliff and kill the twin gods that lived in the underground there.

The brothers returned as they had been advised and killed a great many cave dwellers. But after the battles, when they inspected the scalp piles, they did not see any that belonged to the gods. So they called upon Lightning and Bear, who offered help. Two others offered help as well, Turtle and Frog. If anyone could win the enemy gods' scalps, it was they, for they were clever fighters, and well-protected too. When they went into battle, the axe blows of the cave dwellers glanced off Turtle's shell. They tried to burn him, but he just spat out the fire. They tried to boil him in a water jar, but, once inside, Turtle kicked it apart.

The two brothers, along with Frog and Turtle, fought the cave dwellers bravely and well. But finally, elder brother and younger brother were called in—so were the members of the Flint Clan, and so was Old Woman, Mountain Goddess

of Hunger. She proved to be helpful, for while the two
brothers were dancing about the fire with their bodies
daubed in clay, she made it appear that they were merely a
bunch of stars. She herself changed into clouds, raided the
cave dwellers' cornfields, and stole much corn for everyone
to eat.

Now Bear and Snake were in on this fight, but they had
not yet really shown themselves. They sat and talked and
smoked, while the others went out and fought. Then, when
the time was right, they stole away and found the House of
the Enemy. There, they spied two gods, crawling about on
hands and knees. Bear killed one with his tongue and Snake
killed the other with his teeth. Then they skinned the gods,
took their hearts out, and rode away on their ponies of
sunlight-and-wind.

Then Bear and Snake made a circular house. Bear sat on
the white side of the house, smoking his white shell pipe.
Snake sat on the black side of the house, smoking his turquoise pipe. Bear's tobacco pouch had a sun on it, Snake's
had a moon. They smoked very sweet tobacco.

Two pretty girls were filling their water jars at the river
and they smelled the sweet smoke. The smoke came out
of the roof of the hogan of Bear and Snake. The girls followed the smoke which led them to the two handsome
old men.

"I would like to have some of your smoke," the older sister
said to Bear.

Bear said, "Where do you come from?"

"I come from the mountain."

"And I come," the younger sister said to Snake, "from the
plain."

"Sit by me," Bear said to the older one.

"Sit by me," Snake said to the younger.

And the girls soon smoked the pipes of the two old

warriors, but the tobacco was strong and it put them to sleep. In the morning they saw who they had slept with, and they ran away. But Bear and Snake caught up with them and gave each a present: a sacred basket. When they got into trouble, all they had to do was stand in the basket, and it would take them away from danger. The girls went back to their village.

But when they got there, they found that the villagers were angry with them. The villagers started to whip them, but the girls got into their baskets and flew away. The older flew to the mountains, the younger to the plain.

Now, the elder sister ran until she came to the place of holy mountains. There, a chipmunk took pity on her and brought her to a cave. Inside the cave, Talking God took her to a holy room where the First Earth People lived. Bear's guardian, Lightning, was there, and Talking God sprinkled cornmeal on him and said the prayer of protection.

The elder sister stayed with the First Earth People for a long time. She had a girl baby there, and it was born with dark fur all over its body, but its face was white and clean. The elder sister went on many journeys all around.

PART TWO

She traveled to Rio Grande Canyon where she ate corn mush cooked in green leaves by Mountain Hunger Goddess. She traveled south to Sante Fe Mountain where the Turquoise Clan gave her a ceremony. At La Bajada Hill she met the Bluebird People and at Sandia Mountain she met the people who later moved to Hopi. At Las Lunas she met the Deer People, at Laguna the Mountain Sheep People.

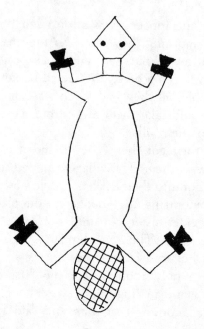

Beaver.

She met the Beavers at Jemez and the Dancing Bears at Mount Taylor.

She saw the Mountain Jay People dancing at Acoma and then she went further west and met the Squirrel People. On the mountain southwest of Zuni she met more Bear People. While she was there, she saw the Garden of Lightning, full of squash and beans.

Then she learned things she would later need to know: Water Monster taught her medicine, and the Porcupine Clan up in the San Francisco Peaks showed her how to make coats. At the Place of the Chief of the Birds she heard Robin's big speech and she met Changing Bear Maiden, the Bear Sister whose husband was Coyote, and while there, she learned Bear Sister's true name was Sickness.

After many adventures and much traveling, she came to Horse Lake for a bath and then back to the place known as Wide Berries, which was the home of the Bears, where she lay down to rest.

PART THREE

Later on, the elder sister, who is now known as Bear Woman, married a man at Kintyel and had a son by him. There was a terrible drought at that time, and all the people around there moved away. But Bear Woman and her husband and son stayed on.

One day Bear Woman was trapped in her hogan by a starved mother bear. She and her husband managed to escape, leaving their infant son swinging from a cradleboard tied to the roof beam. The starved mother bear took the child and nursed it in her den north of Ignacio. She brought him to that den, taught him the ways of the bears, and how to listen to what the wind says.

Then another drought and famine struck the land, and the boy, who was now twelve years old, was afraid that his adoptive mother, the bear, would try and eat him. The wind warned him that this was so, so he escaped, but for four days the mother bear chased after him. Wherever he ran, the wind warned him, telling him to climb up a cactus, run into a cave, hide behind a big tree. . . .

So, in that way, he kept out of her sight, until the fourth day when she said, "I will hunt you no more." Then she told him to find his real mother and she gave him a prayerstick covered with feathers and a long stick wound with cotton.

The last thing she did was give him four secret names that can only be spoken in winter.

The boy looked for his real mother and found her. He

grew up and married. His second wife abandoned their child. This is what happened.

PART FOUR

He had large round eyes and his fingers where sharp like claws.

He liked to grab things, and hold them tight to his chest. Second Wife was afraid of the child, she hung his cradle-board in a piñon tree, and forgot about him. Mother Owl heard the child cry and took him to her hollow tree.

He grew up like an owl. He could swoop low when he ran with his arms out; he could tear meat from bones.

One day Owl Mother said, "You should go find your real mother, the one who put you in the tree where I found you, my son."

Owl Boy agreed and went to find his first family. He traveled four days, and on the fourth night, he found a hogan with a familiar smell, but no one lived in it anymore.

But a corncob lying in the ashes spoke to him, told him where to go. He found his mother and father at a big dance, the whole tribe was there, dancing. He went to them but they were afraid of him: his big eyes, his long sharp finger-nails, his voice that sounded like the wind playing a flute in a hollow tree.

Then the dancers shot arrows at him, and he shot arrows back at them, and he killed some of them, before they scattered.

He ran away from them and lived by himself for a time, but he always dreamed of seeing his real mother again.

One day he found a hogan with a familiar smell, and a fire-poker lying in the ashes of the outside fireplace said: "Go inside, you will see your mother there."

He went inside and saw his mother making a basket. She did not know who he was, but his father and the other children knew him.

That night his father took him to a dance. While he was there, he shot a blind old man. The next night, he shot an old woman. The next night, he shot a little boy. The next night, a little girl.

Then the clan chased him off, threatening him. The wind told him that it would be dangerous to stay and he went south to the river and escaped.

PART FIVE

In time, Owl Boy's two younger brothers grew up and became wicked. One day the elder brother was captured by the Utes. The chief later adopted him and raised him as his own son. When the elder brother turned twenty-four, he was made a chief himself. In his chief's tent he kept a string of:

> Eagle feathers pointing east
> Hawk feathers pointing south
> Woodpecker feathers pointing west
> Magpie feathers pointing north

One day the Utes went off on a hunt, but the elder brother stayed behind. He needed some feathers to make arrows with, so he plucked a few of the sacred feathers from the roof of his tipi. This caused great unrest with the Utes when they found out. A council was held to decide how to punish their chief for plucking the sacred feathers. They decided to make him a slave and then kill him.

That day he was sent to the river with water jars. Bending

down to fill them, he knew, then and there, on that day he would die.

Staring at the moving water, he started to prepare himself. Just then, something fell from the sky and landed in the water in front of him. It was a little basket with a prayerstick in it.

The elder brother picked it out of the water, and a man appeared before him. The man was named Holy Mountain Man.

"Boy Chief," the holy person addressed him, "Do you know you are going to die?"

"I do."

"And do you know where the Utes keep their treasure?"

"I do."

"Then you must go there."

"Why should I do this, if they are going to kill me?"

"Do it," Holy Mountain Man said, "and something will happen."

Then the holy one disappeared and the elder brother returned to the camp with the water jars full of water. In front of his tipi, a guard stood watch. The elder brother heard the sound of pottery drums, telling of his death.

It was summer, the leaves of the trees were green. Then the drums fell silent. He waited, wondering. There was a chill in the air. The elder brother wrapped himself in a buffalo robe, and looked out of the tipi flap. The guard was no longer there. Out of the clear blue sky came clouds. It started to snow. There were flakes, fluffy and white, like moths. Soon the earth was white and the Utes were inside their tipis, trying to stay warm.

The elder brother remembered what he was supposed to do. Slipping unnoticed out of his tipi, he went to the secret cave where the Utes kept sacred stones, cottons, skins, buckskins, and war bonnets. These he took up in his arms, and went out into the softly falling snow. Walking, he dropped things, for there was too much to hold in his arms. But Holy Mountain Man appeared again and made the treasures of the Utes so small they fit into the elder brother's medicine pouch. Then, he left the camp, traveling lightly.

The following day, he was making good time, but a Ute war party was not far behind. He did not think he could outrun them.

Then Talking God appeared. "Remember," he said, "the Animal People will protect you." The elder brother traveled on until he came to a river.

The Utes were only a few steps behind him when a voice said: "Come into my home and you will be safe." And the river lifted like a blue blanket and the elder brother went under it into the home of the otter.

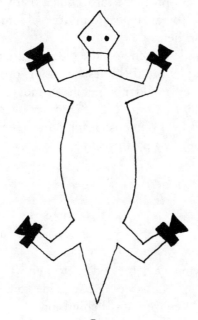

Otter.

"Here," the elder brother said, "take what you wish. . . ." He opened his medicine bag and Otter took a blue stone and thanked him.

The next day, the elder brother made good time, but the Utes stayed on his trail. He reached a ridge, they were right behind, he could see the dust-clouds made by their moccasins. I am lost now, he thought, surely they will find me.

But Wind came to him, then, and dusted his tracks so that they disappeared and then Wind raised clouds of dust and the Utes could not see anything. The elder brother was thankful and offered his medicine bag to Wind who took paint for his face and some curing herbs.

The day after this, the elder brother was caught by the Utes, and they were about to kill him. They had tied him to a rock. The elder brother heard a voice that squeaked in his ear. Pack Rat Woman appeared in front of him. "Quick," she said, "Come in here."

The rock rolled open and the elder brother fell into the hole. He could hear the Utes knocking on it with their lances, but they could not get it to move. She fed him cornmeal and yucca fruit. He offered her his medicine bag: She took a little ground squirrel skin. Then she danced about her cave, singing this song:

> Ground Squirrel used to be my neighbor,
> used to be my neighbor
> he lived next door
> he lived next door—

The following day, the elder brother was chased until sundown by the Ute scalping party. He came to a canyon wall and the Utes were just behind him.

If I jump off, he thought, I will break every bone.

Spider Woman came to him, then: "Hang down on my little thread," she said. And he did. Afterward he offered her his medicine bag, and she took a ball of cotton yarn. The Utes had to go the long way around and into the canyon. But they managed to do this very quickly, and they caught up to the elder brother and pinned him to a dead juniper tree.

The elder brother prepared to die, but just then, a hollow voice said to him: "Climb into the tree and I will protect you."

He climbed into the juniper and Owl flew over it four times and sprinkled medicine on the branches, and the Utes hunted around the tree. But the elder brother had become as thin as the moonlight and they could not see him. He offered Owl his medicine bag, but she said she did not need anything.

The next day the elder brother walked across Rainbow Bridge with Holy Mountain Man and they went all the way to Shiprock. The elder brother opened his bag. All that was left was a war bonnet, which Holy Mountain Man took.

And the Utes turned back and went home, empty-handed.

PART SIX

After his adventure with the Utes, the elder brother journeyed to Beautiful Mountain. He climbed until he came to a hogan. Two bears guarded the entrance, but when they saw him they let him pass. He went inside and saw a bear sitting in front of the fire.

"Do you want some berries to eat?" the bear asked.

He was ready to reach out for them when his prayerstick said: "Accept only cornmeal with salt."

Then the bear offered him some cornmeal with salt, and he gratefully took it.

After he had eaten, the bear said: "Let me show you your room."

There was a bear den to the east. As they headed for it, the prayerstick said: "Do not sleep there."

"Is there another place I could sleep?" the elder brother asked.

The bear showed him another den toward the south. The walls were covered with cedar bark. Again, the prayerstick said: "Do not sleep there."

He was shown another den covered in pine boughs, and the prayerstick warned him against that one, too.

At last Bear Woman came and showed him a den to the north where everything was arranged properly:

Black bear pelts on the east wall
Red pelts on the south wall
White pelts on the west wall
Many-colored pelts on the north wall

In the center of the den there was a bed made of buffalo hide. The sun came in from the west wall and lit a thin pane of mica. The room looked bright and warm.

Bear Woman told him, "If you wish to sleep in darkness, motion to Sun and Mica, and the room will grow dark."

The elder brother was tired from all his journeys. He motioned to Sun and Mica, the room darkened. He slept.

In the morning there was an earthquake which woke the Bear People. The elder brother got up and bathed in a basket with fir-branches all around it. When he stepped out, the water dripped off him and the bears dried him all over with cornmeal. Then they washed and combed his hair, and he ate a breakfast of cornmeal mush.

Afterward, he showed them his medicine bag. Deep
within he found some gifts for the bears: tobacco, buckskin
dresses, flutes, and whistles. The Bear People praised these
gifts and made the elder brother feel well.

Then they said good-bye to him and he went on his way.
As usual, Talking God looked after him.

The prayerstick foretold what would happen: Soon Holy
Maiden would come and she would greet the elder brother
in a shaft of rain. He would then give her a gift of buckskin
and she would promise to come again. Then a cloud would
come, she would step in it and go away.

All this happened as the prayerstick said it would. The
elder brother then climbed a hill of yellow grass. The wind
struck him four times. Talking God took him to the Council
Place. To the Holy People assembled there, he gave the
contents of his medicine bag.

Then he took off his clothes and sat down on a small sand
painting. The Frog People came in, sat down all around him,
and started croaking. The elder brother shivered, the frogs
went away. The medicine man walked back and forth. The
elder brother felt better.

Then they went into a medicine hogan. Inside there was
another sand painting, on buckskin. And a second one,
showing all of the gifts given to the Holy People, and the
whole story of his journey.

Three ceremonies were held over the elder brother, and
a messenger was sent to each of the four sacred mountains.

The fourth ceremony had the arrow painting in it. The
elder brother was the first Indian ever to learn it. He was
told that the first dancers were birds, insects, and animals.

Other ceremonies were given:

He was striped black and spotted like a snake
He was painted red
He was cured of evil and evil dreams
He was given pure thoughts, a pure body
He was told medicine that he would always have
He was told to teach his younger brother the Way
He was told it would take him five years
He was told to give the ceremonies only after the
    first frost.

After the elder brother taught his younger brother everything he needed to know to become a medicine man, he went away. We know where he went. The Holy People took him back to the Bear People on Black Mountain.

He is there to this day, so they say.

THE
BEADWAY

Eagle.

The Beadway is a myth that celebrates the spirit of the eagle. In a songlike style the storyteller takes his young hero up into the cliffs and places him in the nest of the eagles. Here he must prove to the Mother and Father Eagle that he is worthy of their trust, which he achieves by being kindly to their young ones. For his goodness of heart, they take him into the sky above the clouds to the land of the eagle spirits.

Once in sky country, his troubles begin. For the seemingly human curse of curiosity is his undoing. The youth is warned to stay in Eagle Chief's house, but he cannot resist going outside and meeting a "funny animal" who turns out to be Coyote. Once bewitched, the youth is taught the ceremony that undoes Coyote's evil spell, but later on the boy gets curious again and goes out peering into the many-colored homes of the Eagle People. This time he gets wounded with Spirit Arrows and becomes sick.

The story shows the stages of the hero's sickness and the ceremony by which Eagle Chief cures him. In the Blessing-way and the Flintway the healing process depicts the shattered state of the hero after the spell is cast and we are told how he is made whole again. In the Beadway the source of healing is the familiar hoops and the rite of passing through them is symbolic of going through the stages of an illness and coming out clean. Yet in the Beadway it is the little downy emblem of the eagle, the symbol of breath, that the medicine man uses along with the mature feather of an eagle to recondition the mind and body and consummate the cure. There is a Navajo song that celebrates eagle power:

> Now The People will wear your claws on their chest,
> Your feathers will hang in their hogan,
>
> The People will dance with your wings and see with
> Your eyes: You belong now, to The People.

In former times the Beadway was used as a panacea for such illnesses as boils, sores, sore throat, swollen legs, vomiting, itching, and scalp, hair, and head soreness. Today, it might be impossible to find anyone on the reservation who uses the Beadway to treat these ailments. It is as if the myth had survived through the art of storytelling to impart only the spiritual message that was once part of the medicinal cure. If the medicine men who once practiced this Way are gone, so (almost) is the great bird that inspired it.

But the myth lives on, as alive today as when the people in the story were asked to shed their beads, bracelets, turquoise, and silver (there was, and still is, a necessary tribute for the calling of a Way). Although the tribe is sorry to lose its jewelry, the moral is implicit: something given, something taken. They have given up their goods in exchange for taking the Beadway with them. And the hero, before leaving the people to go up into the sky, makes a promise: "I will always be with you from above, watching over you, and the ceremony." In no other story does the storyteller put his hero's faith so devotedly in words.

The dust of the eagle's wing was once thought to contain so much power that, if shaken into a person's face, it would cause blindness. This is why, in Part One of the tale, the villagers fall down, stricken by eagle-wing dust, unable to move. The power of the eagle, like the bear, is not confined to the belief of the Navajo. Some North American tribes formed entire religions around the eagle. Virtually all have made use of its feathers and claws. The greatest test of bravery a Native American warrior might endure was to face a bear and kill it, or to capture and kill an eagle. The wearing of feather and claw was a testament to the man who wore it, a form of rank that would often stop a fight rather than provoke it.

The earlier myths in this book began in darkness and progressed into the light. The Beadway passes the listener above the earth and up into the spirit realm. We go "through the hole in the sky" and to the opposite end of the nadir, heaven. But what we discover through the eyes of the hero is that, underneath the feather cloaks of the eagles, are naked-skinned human beings just like us. The moral then pulls us full circle: from the depths to the heights, only to find out at the very upper reaches of the sky that there are wars there the same as on earth—and the Eagle Chief is just as vexed by this as the first Earth Surface Man.

There was a boy, one of the Creation People, who lived at Mount Taylor. One day he was out at Pueblo Bonito, hunting for seeds, when two hunters came upon him. They captured the boy and took him back with them to Aztec where they kept him prisoner for four days.

At the end of that time, they told the boy to go down to the San Juan River. There was a cliff there, they said, where the eagles lived. "Go back and bring us two nestlings." If he brought them what they wanted, they promised to give him food and water.

Now the people from Aztec followed the boy to the cliff of the eagle nestlings. "Here is a basket," they told him. "When you get to the nest, put the two nestlings in this basket. Then lower it down to us."

The boy said he would do this, and he started to climb to the top of the cliff. When he got to the nest, he saw that it was partially hidden inside a cave. There was a large boulder in front that he had to crawl around. Soon he was out of sight to the people below who were watching him.

Once inside the cave, the boy made his way to the nest where he saw the two baby eagles. But while he was crawling, Wind told him: "Do not take the little eagles."

He moved forward and Dragonfly flew in front of his face: "Do not take them or you will stay here forever and turn into dust."

The boy listened to these words of warning, but he still inched forward. When he reached the nestlings, they backed away from him.

"When do your parents return?" he asked them.

"Dawn," they answered.

After a time, night came to the cliff and it grew dark. The boy shivered in the cold. The eaglets put on four robes. First, they put on Darkness, then Morning Dawn, then Yellow Afterglow, and finally, Blue Afterglow. The boy was cold so he slept on the edge of the robes.

At Morning Dawn, Father Eagle flew into the cave. He

saw the boy sleeping beside his young ones. "You did not steal my children," he said to the boy.

"No, I did not."

"You must be hungry."

The boy said that he was. Father Eagle gave him a yellow bowl of cornmeal mush, which he took from under his right wing. The boy began to eat hungrily, stabbing at the mush with one finger.

"You must not eat that way," Eagle father said.

So the boy used two fingers to eat the mush.

Again, Eagle Father scolded him and the boy ate with three fingers. When he was scolded a third time, the boy used four fingers, but Eagle Father said: "You must eat with your whole hand."

The boy finished eating.

Father Eagle said, "I will return in four days and we will talk, then, about what to do."

Soon after he flew away, Mother Eagle arrived. She saw that the boy had not harmed her young ones, and she treated him as Father Eagle had done, with kindness and respect. She offered him many-colored cornmeal and promised to return in three days.

When she left, the boy watched a basket come down from above on a rope. He knew that there were people above him and below him, and they wanted him to bring the nestlings out now. He did not know what to do. Then one of the nestlings came forward. It walked unsteadily to the edge of the cave mouth, then it flapped its wings vigorously, and a strange dust went up and down, floating on the breeze. The people below caught the dust in their eyes, and were blinded. The people above passed out and fell off the cliff.

After a time, when the people below could see again, they vowed to shoot the boy with arrows and kill him. They took their places and waited for him to show himself.

Then Morning Dawn came, and with it Father Eagle. Shortly after that, Mother Eagle came.

Father Eagle said, "The people await you with bows and arrows. You must escape before it is too late."

"How should I escape?" the boy asked.

"There are Eagle People on the cliff above us, waiting for you."

The boy looked out of the cave. The Eagle People had lowered robes to hide him in:

> *Darkness robe*
> *Morning dawn robe*
> *Afterglow robe*
> *Blue afterglow robe*

Then the boy climbed into the robes, which Father Eagle and Mother Eagle wrapped around him. They gave him a quartz crystal which lit up the darkness of the robes and a horn with twelve holes in it through which he could breathe. Then they carried him above to the other Eagle People, who took hold of the robes with their beaks.

Singing and flapping, singing and shaking, they took hold of the robes and began to rise up into the air. Higher and higher, making a big circle they flew to Huerfano Mountain, then down to the mesa below Pueblo Bonito. They went north to a point of rock near Thoreau and to San Anton Spring where The People get their white paint. They left there and flew to Mount Taylor, then into the sky. But the boy was heavy, they fell back down and had to go up again. Then Chicken Hawk flew through a little opening in the sky. "Get help from the Sky People," the eagles called and Chicken Hawk brought back Blue Racer and Black Racer Snake; they wrapped their tails around Eagle Boy's head and pulled him through the hole in the sky.

The boy was brought out of the robes and he watched as the Eagle People took off their feather-clothes and hung them on a tree. Underneath their feathers, he saw that they were human, just like him.

The Bird People lived in many houses in the sky:

> *East of the big black eagles*
> *South house of the hawks*
> *West house of the yellow-tailed eagles*
> *North house of eagles, buzzards, and other birds*

The boy was asked to stay at White House, with a chief. But the first morning there, he saw a funny animal sitting on a shelf of rock. It was Coyote, but the boy did not recognize him. When he walked over to see what it was, Coyote struck at the boy's shoulder. This turned him into a coyote.

That night the Eagle People went out looking for the boy, but they only found a poor skinny coyote, walking around.

Dragonfly said, "That is the boy."

Wind said, "It is."

So the Eagle People put the boy through sacred hoops and changed him back into himself.

The next morning they warned him to stay put, but he went over to Blue House instead. There, he saw four water jars. By mistake, he tipped one over on its side and a black cloud came out of it. Then a big rain soaked the boy to the bone.

That night, when the Eagle People returned they saw what had happened. One of them set the water jug upright, and it stopped raining.

The next morning, the boy went to the river, where he saw Frog and Toad. They had their Spirit Arrows ready, and they shot him full of them. From that moment on, the boy could not move.

But the Eagle People cured him with medicine and they pulled out the Spirit Arrows that were stuck in his body.

The fourth morning, the boy was curious, as usual. He went over to visit the black and white striped houses of the Eagles and Buzzards. Their guard shot arrows at him. From that moment on, the boy felt sick.

It took longer for the Eagle People to heal him, but after a full night of prayer and medicine, he was back in good health.

The next morning the Eagle Chief told the boy to stay at home. But when the people went off, as they did every morning, he was curious, and followed them. As he was walking along, he heard a small voice say, "sh, sh." This was Spider Man, speaking from his little house in the ground.

"Why do the people go to the east every morning?" the boy asked.

"They are having a war," Spider Man said.

"Who do they fight with—?"

"They fight with Bumblebees, Honeybees, and Swallows."

"Are the Eagle People winning?" the boy asked.

"They are losing. And there is a weed that is crushing them. It rolls all around, killing them."

"Can anything be done?" the boy said.

Spider Man replied, "There is something ... here, take my cane and this eagle-down feather."

"What shall I do with them?"

"The cane will bring the people back to life and the feather will take you anywhere you want to go."

"Is that all you wish to tell me?" the boy questioned.

"There is one thing more," Spider Man said. "Use this rabbitbrush to strike the enemy: It will kill them."

"How many must I kill?"

"You should kill all the bees, except for one male and one

female. The dangerous weed is medicine, you must capture it. One day the people will need to use it."

The boy did as he was told. He killed all but two bees, which he saved for the people to be used as medicine. He caught the dangerous weed, and saved it for healing. As a result of killing these enemies, the Eagle People made him Eagle Chief and taught him all of their dances, prayers, sand paintings, and songs. It took him many years to learn the Eagle Chant, but finally he learned it and became a great medicine man.

In time, he taught his younger brother the ceremonies of the eagles. This was done on top of Mount Taylor:

Eagle Chief took all the bracelets, beads, belts, and turquoise that The People had to give. He told his brother not to stop singing, dancing. His brother sang and danced. The dancing and the singing lifted Eagle Chief into the sky. Higher and higher, he went up. "I will always be with you," he said, "watching over your ceremony."

Then he went up out of sight. The People started yelling because their beads and bracelets were gone. That is why they call it the Beadway. The people lost all their fine jewelry, but they decided that was all right because they had something even more valuable than silver and turquoise. They had Eagle Chief looking over them. That is what they say, anyway.

THE
BLUEJAY WAY

The Navajo Ways are a series of interrelated origin myths. Where and when they began, no one really knows. But we do know that bits and pieces of the myths have come from sources other than Navajo experience. One can see Pueblo influences in many of the tales, and certainly echoes of the Southern Plain tribes.

How does a myth begin?

It must come from human experience, the kind that teaches us how to survive. As a Sioux man once told me: "Our ancient stories were told to our young to protect them. That is their real virtue."

Here, then, is a Navajo origin myth that is not hundreds of years old. It is perhaps about thirty years old, and it is the spiritual story of a Navajo man who learned from his father how to become a member of the tribe. This was something that he had always taken for granted, but upon graduating from college and entering "the white man's world," he discovered he was suddenly on different ground. His Navajo friends shied away from him. Perhaps it was on account of those four years being away at college. But maybe he just looked and acted like another person. Something of the larger world had rubbed off on him. He no longer rode his horse on the hills, he no longer took pride in the old ways, the old songs.

As he put it himself: "After graduation I was ready to go for whatever was out there. But I wasn't ready to use my education; I didn't really know how to put it to use. I remember standing in the post office one day, and an old friend, one of my high school buddies, came up to me and started up a conversation.

"'So,' he said, 'You've got that big degree.'

"*I was wondering what else he was going to say. You see, I was the one who went away, who went off chasing some pretty big scheme. Not all kids who go to high school on the reservation have the chance of going to college. In my community, I was the first one. . . .*

"*But he said something like this—'You're not one of The People anymore. You don't even have a horse, you're not mobile.'*

"*I stayed up nights, thinking of what he said, for he didn't say it in a mean way. But it was hard-sounding, the way it came out. He just meant that as a Navajo, I wasn't as important as I thought I was. I had the college degree, all right, but in the process, I'd lost . . . well, to put it the only way I know how, I'd lost my Navajoness, my mobility.*

"*You see, there is nothing more important to a Navajo than being mobile. That is what took us out of bondage, the freedom to travel across miles of desert, free as the wind. He'd hit on something big in my life. I now saw myself a little differently. I was not so important anymore.*

"*Oh, I had a horse—the one my parents gave me for high school graduation. But I didn't ride it anymore. Then something magical happened to me, something that taught me who I was, who I was going to be.*

"*My father says it's necessary to wait until one can carry the word properly—that is, if one has any words to carry. Do you know what I mean? You must wait until there is some snow on the mountain. . . .*"

By which he meant the white hair on the top of his head, which, in the Navajo culture is a sign of wisdom.

"*For many years,*" *he went on,* "*I have chased after a horse that is only half-real . . . a horse made of flesh and bone, a horse made of myths. Just as I have had to learn the Beautyway, I have had to puzzle out the meaning of that horse. And it's taken me half a lifetime.*"

Then he told the story of his life. As he talked, he spun

into and out of the Beautyway myths, weaving them skill-
fully into his own narrative.

This was the apocryphal tale of the Sun Horse that the
Sun Father rides across the sky, while carrying the sun.
The Sun Father has five horses, he explained. An albino
horse, symbolizing dawn; a blue roan for the turquoise sky
of noon; a red chestnut horse for sundown; a dark bay
horse for night. The fifth horse is representative of the un-
chosen horse to be ridden by the Sun's son when he
comes to visit.

The Bluejay Way, then, is one man's story of how he
came to know himself—by knowing his place of origin.
Riding in the afternoon, a dust storm on the horizon, he sees
that speck which is himself, dust, on the wind of a clear
summer day. Even dust has a place of holiness. For, as The
People say, "mist on the horizon is the pollen of the gods."
As the speck of dust grew larger, he saw himself upon a
horse not his own, a horse of magnificence.

In giving himself back to The People, to the traditional
Ways of the Navajo, the man gave himself, as a gift, back to
himself. The two worlds that he had been living in—one
white and one Indian—came together, just as the horse of
dreams, of myth, became flesh.

So it was in the beginning when the Ways, the stories of
origin, were first told. From a single happening there sprang
a fountain of storytelling, a sudden flow of language and
metaphor, meaning and message. Out of a single track in the
sand came the wings of the first butterfly and a galloping
fire-white horse that could walk on clouds.

There was a place he knew, a sacred butte, miles from his
family's ranch. It was out there in the cedarland where The
People did the Rain-praying Ceremony, Rainy Butte.

Saddling the old horse given to him by his mother for the trip, he rode off in the direction of a dream, not knowing what he would find, a piece of memory, maybe.

Twelve men had gone up Rainy Butte. Twelve men, a young boy, a young girl. The boy was himself, the girl, some- one he knew. And the men were elders of the tribe. He was the water-carrier; she was the cornmeal-carrier. He carried the black waterjar and she carried the basket. And all the time they walked up Rainy Butte, the lead singer at the head of the line of men sang the songs of rain.

He remembered all of it. The night's wait in the tipi- hogan made of plants, the center poles made of trees. All night there was singing in the pinetree-sprucetree house, with the roots turned up to the sky. Before dawn, they left that place and went up Rainy Butte. He was Corn Boy, she was Corn Girl. And the twelve elders were like the twelve Yei, or Holy People. Up into the Navajo dawn they walked, solemnly, their footsteps like prayers.

At the top of Rainy Butte, he remembered, you could see Mount Taylor to the south; Mount Hesperus to the north; Mount Blanco to the east; the San Francisco Peaks to the west. If you could not see them, you could, if your heart was strong, feel them.

But all that had happened many years ago. What did he feel now as he rode to the foot of Rainy Butte? One thing his father had said, before he left this time: "Do not be afraid of what you may see up there on top." That was all he had said. It was enough.

Above all he knew the rules to abide. Wait for the rising sun. Do not show fear. Expect nothing, keep an open mind, be still, face east. For, as he well knew, the gods did not often bless the wary, the fearful, the careless, or the proud. They gave their blessings to the simple of heart, the strong of heart, those who could wait.

Until now his life had been a shambles. College had given,

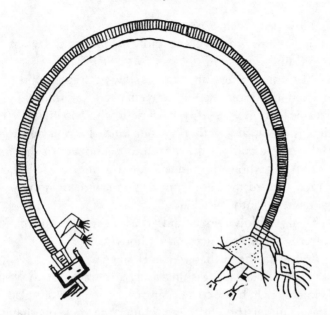

Rainbow.

and taken. It had given him knowledge, but it had taken his soul. Now, riding into the valley of dreams, he saw himself redeemed. He saw his life take shape before his eyes. Riding the rough trail to Rainy Butte, he felt the light sprinkle of rain. For a while, the gentle needles tickled his face and wetted his horse. He rode on, thinking. Then the rain let up, the sun came out. The sky went aqua, a coppery green. The damp cedars burned green in the subterranean glow, and a short rainbow glittered the valley with slabs of primary light.

Suddenly, looking down in the glare, he saw them: tracks of the Sun Horse in the wet sand. Seeing the little wing-shapes of the unshod horse reminded him of the story his father told, the legend of the Sun Horse, how it came to life.

When the Holy People first made the horse, it was a complete thing, but it would not come to life. They tried to get it to rise up on its strong legs, but it would not rise. Caterpillar was asked to help.

"How can I help?" he asked.

"You know," one of the Holy People said, "where the sacred flints are kept."

"Yes, this is true. But I am so slow getting around."

Then the Holy People prayed over Caterpillar and he became Butterfly. Swiftly he flew to the Mountain Where Flint Is Kept, and gathering four flints, he returned to the Holy People and put the flints into the hooves of the horse.

The great horse stirred, quivered, came to life. Then it surged, leaped into life, struck the air with its hooves, and galloped off into the clouds.

"Look," a Holy Person said, "the horse makes the marks of Butterfly when it dances on its hooves."

And it has been that way ever since.

It rained all day, washing away the tracks of the horse. Tying his own horse to a cedar tree, he found a dry place for himself under the cliff edge. Under the rock overhang he made a fire and hung his wet clothes on cedar sticks to dry them out. Night came on, the moon and rolling clouds passed over his head. Wrapped up in a warm blanket, his round-topped, flat-brimmed Stetson pulled down over his eyes, he hardly knew if he slept or remained awake. The wind came up and brought with it a spice-breath of wet sage. Wind, in the old stories, was always a messenger. Hidden under his hat, he wondered, now, if wind was trying to tell him something.

He felt a chill on the back of his neck. There was a whispering that was not wind. Then he heard voices, one Spanish, one American. Different-sounding ways of talking: one that slipped, soft; one that skimmed like a flat rock on a pond. Wind, the messenger, brought the voices to him now. He got up from the fire, and stepping free of his blanket, put on the half-dry clothes. The jeans were stiff and damp.

The men, he judged, were quite close to his camp. Stealthily, he crept up on the ridge, dodging the broad but irregular swaths of moonlight. Finally, when he gained the crest of the ridge, he saw them, the whisperers on the wind.

There was a lone cedar in the moon on the top of the ridge. An owl, sitting on a dead branch, was whispering to a coyote, sitting on moonlit haunches under the tree. Their voices came clearly to him as he lay on his belly, listening to them talk. He did not wait around, but drew back silently, brushing his footprints with a cedar bough. When he got back to the campfire, he heaped deadwood on it, building the flames into a small bonfire that lapped at the edges of the rock cove where he had made his camp.

Crouching by the fire, his horse saddled and ready to ride, the reins in his hand, he waited out the night. Sometimes, restless dreams came after him, but he shook them off, staying awake. Warnings, like woodrats, scampered through the thoughtless bin of his brain—he chased them out.

In the early hours before the dawn, he drifted off. A voice said to him: "If a man counts out his days, he will die."

"I haven't done that," he said out loud.

The voice said, "If a man whistles in the dark, ghosts will haunt him."

"I never whistled."

Then: "If you dream your horse is dead, you will die."

"I've chased away evil dreams."

"If someone pulls your teeth in a dream—"

"I've had no dreams—" He jumped to his feet. It was nearly dawn. Facing east, he rode into the chilly morning. As he rode away from the ridge, he thought he heard something tinkling musically in the air. Too cold for Hummingbird, he mused. He craned his neck, looked back at the lone cedar. The unholy pair were gone. But in the steely light of dawn, he saw a pair of ancient spurs twinkling silver on the fading moon. He shivered and rode on.

Riding into the first light of the sun, he said the morning prayer of *hozhoni*:

May all be well above me
May all be well below me
May all be well all around me
The sky, be well
The earth, be well
The light, the darkness
The mystery that is fire
The prayer that is water
In harmony it is done
In harmony, it is finished
May harmony be all around me
All the days of my life

Memory brought it back: the old trail of childhood, up the foot of Rainy Butte. Tying his horse to a tree, he took it on foot. The climb was much harder than he remembered. His legs were older, less sure of themselves. As he climbed, he blessed his legs, his feet, his boots. And climbing, kept climbing.

What he found, he knew: the trail back into himself, the jagged rocks, the slippery jointed cracks, the slick cobble, the falling-off places.

At the top, in the dawn sun, he prayed again:

I walk in plain sight of my home
I am at the entrance of my home
I am in the middle of my home
I am at the back of my home
I am at the top of the pollen footprint
Before me it is beautiful
Behind me it is beautiful
Under me it is beautiful
Above me it is beautiful
All around me it is beautiful

He felt himself rising and expanding with the words of the prayer. He felt the world echo with this expansion. The brightness all around him turned brighter. And something happened. His father's words came back to him: "Don't be afraid of what you see up there."

The horse came suddenly out of the sun. A golden horse with a mane of sun rays, with feet of flint butterflies that clattered on the clouds. It came out of the sun and thundered upon the clouds, and kicked lightning loose on the world. He trembled at the sight of it.

It came right at him, its nostrils flaring, an aura of pollen shining around its head, a song coming from its hooves, a dancing, wild, prancing, golden horse with a wildflower hanging from the corner of its mouth.

It galloped at him. He closed his eyes, praying softly. The horse was almost on him, he could feel its oncoming surge, the force of its body moving through the light of morning. It will crush me, he thought, it will surely crush my bones to dust. But his father's words returned to him, again and again, until he was repeating them like a chant.

Then he closed his eyes and the horse came on into the night of his head, a sunbeam in its mouth for a bridle. He wanted to dive under its terrible hooves, but he held to the vow of his father's words. Sucking his breath deep within the cave of his bones, he released his fear; he gave out a great shuddering of breath into the morning air. His shoulders fell, his head drooped.

And the horse of the sun passed lightly through him. He felt it enter him, go through him, go beyond him. He opened his eyes: The horse was going down the steep trail to the foot of Rainy Butte.

He saw the golden-white of its tail flick furiously as it danced down the rocky trail, a cloud of dust rising in its wake.

In the gentle rain that fell after it was gone, he sang the song of the Sun Father's horse.

Hear his whinny now—
The horse of heaven,
Sun Father's horse

See him feed on flowers now—
The horse of the Sun
Whose butterfly hooves
Dance upon a cloud

Watch him disappear now—
Sun Father's horse
Into the mists of sacred pollen

Hidden, he is hidden
Hear, now, his neigh
Sparkling water falls from his face
Dust of glittering grains
Rises at his hooves

Hidden, he is hidden
Deep within us
The horse of heaven
The Sun Father's horse

Sun.

AFTERWORD:
THE WAYS TODAY

A few years ago, as I began preparations for this book, a Navajo friend warned me that the work was not going to be easy because of the scarcity of available information on the subject.

"The Ways," he said, "are being forgotten faster than they are being remembered."

I asked if, in his opinion, the Ways would last through the next generation of Navajos.

"Well," he said sadly, "they will last, in practice, only as long as The People need them."

"How many old people on the reservation know the Beadway?" I asked.

"Not many. You see, it is not really needed anymore. Not like the Beautyway or some of The Holyway chants. But even those. . . ."

And he went on to tell me of what would happen after his own father died. In a lifetime his father had learned most of the Beautyway chants. Many of these he had told to his son, but how many had he—my friend—successfully passed on to his own children? He couldn't say if they knew any of the actual chants themselves, only the stories or morals he had given to them at certain times in their lives. From what he was saying to me, I intuited that the great draught of Navajo lore fully present in the 1930s was on its way out with the generation who had kept it alive.

I remembered, too, what another Navajo man once told me upon hearing some stories that I had recorded on audio tape for a radio station on the reservation. He said that a lot of Navajo children did not know how to speak Navajo and were, therefore, cut off from their grandparents, some of whom could not tell an origin story without resorting to their own language. "I guess," he had said, "we should be grateful for any way that the words to those old stories come across to the younger generation, for they are not really listening anymore."

I asked my friend what good the stories were without some reference to their historical or ceremonial place.

"You don't know what someone's going to understand," he answered. "It all depends on what they know. I'll tell you something. Since the popularization of movies showing Plains Indians in heroic roles, I've seen a lot of Navajo youth wanting to reject their own heritage and adopt some of the Plains ways, particularly the dancing."

"Is there any interest among the young in Navajo ceremonials?"

"I do not believe so—not much, anyway."

It occurred to me then that what Frank Waters had called "the vast interlocked myth which is at once the complete story of The People and the whole story of man" might be coming to an end.

Some months after our interview in the desert, my friend and his son came to see me. He had some drawings of sand paintings that he wanted to show me. He also brought a drawing of a horseman riding on a ridge at dusk, which he seemed to like. While his young son sat on his lap, he passed the drawing to me. I praised it and put it on the desk between us. Then we got into an animated discussion about the Four Sacred Mountains and our attention turned both inward and outward. He drew a diagram of the mountains and showed me how they represented the four stages of human life, beginning in the east, the mountain of birth, and ending in the north, the mountain of death. While he elaborated, his son picked up a pencil and began to darken the lines of his father's horseman.

"I think he is going to be an artist, like his father," I said.

My friend smiled, made no effort to take the pencil out of his son's hand, though by now, the boy had altered the drawing considerably. Somehow I knew, at that moment, that the Ways would outlast the fear of generational neglect. "There is the song," my friend once said, "and then there is the echo. We like the echo as much as the original song."

By which I understood that the lines his son traced, however crude, were more important to him than his own work. Whatever was passed on, whatever form it might take, was the important thing. For what are the Ways if not the changing forms of a changing people.

GLOSSARY

Animal People In Navajo terms, since animals once talked and moved about like Earth Surface People, they are not regarded as "merely animals." The have a precise identity today that harks back to former times. Today's animals are representative of the original Animal People, who were deities. The myths vary according to the tribe, but the Animal People are always foremost, primary characters on the plane of life. In some cases, an animal appears as the Creator, or as one of the Creator's helpers. The Maidu legend describes a void with no "before" or "after." Out of this falls Silver Fox, the Creator, and Coyote, cocreator and chief antagonist. Thus, the world of the Maidu begins. Many Southwestern Indian legends tell of a world "down-under," a First World of ants, beetles, locusts, and Animal People who "move up" into successive worlds and cocreate the present world we live in now. The Animal People, along with a First Man and First Woman, are responsible for bringing order out of the chaos of the early stages of life on Earth. Most tribes agree that the animals of today are creature-representatives of the original Animal People, whose spirits still inform and guide them. In this sense, the first Animal People are deities, and their ancestral children, the animals around us now, are their spiritual offspring.

Apache The Apaches and the Navajos were once of the same tribe. Both were Athapascan nomads who came down from the cold country of the North. Eventually, the Navajos settled into the Four Corners region where they still live. The Apaches of former times moved about a great deal, being both a mountain and a desert people, and covering an expanse from Mexico to Texas and much of the great Southwest. Noted for their warrior nature, the Apaches were one of the last tribes in America to lay down arms and submit to the reservations designated by the white man.

Bead Before glass beads were introduced by Europeans, Native Americans made beads from quill, shell, bone, horn, and other natural things including seeds, nuts, and roots. Strung together and made into wampum, beads became more than ornamental; they became a part of the economy and were used in trading.

Bear A duality symbol, the bear is both maternal and kind, male-rough and dangerous. By turns, it is also female-vengeful and male-powerful. Native American legends describe bear power as desirable as well as sometimes uncontrollable. Many rites and rituals make the bear into an ally who brings powerful medicine for healing. Bear power comes from the earth. Bear was once assigned by Mother Earth to watch over travelers, those who, like Bear, roam about looking for a place to live.

Bear Woman The elder sister, one of the main characters in the Mountaintop Way, not to be confused with Changing Bear Maiden (in the Moving Up Way), whose husband is Coyote. The latter character is also called Bear's Sister and Sickness.

Bird People All the birds that live in the sky world.

Black Mountain Actual mountain on the Navajo Reservation where bears are said to still inhabit the forests. This was their ancestral home, the place they were banished after giving The People coughing sickness.

Blue Racer Capitalized, this refers to the deity; in lower case, it means any blue racer snake.

Breath Feathers Prayer feathers, usually the downy feathers of the eagle.

Butterfly Due to the natural beauty of its wings, Butterfly is often considered vain. Yet, in Navajo mythology, Butterfly brings the sacred flint to the hooves of the horse. In the legend of the deity, Butterfly Boy was cured of his vanity by being lightning-struck with the axe of Rain Boy. After that, his head opened up and out of it came the butterflies of this world. The perishable dust of Butterfly's wings is sometimes thought to prove that such beauty is usually not durable.

Caterpillar In Navajo belief, Caterpillar is sacred because of his ability to transform into Butterfly, the gatherer of the sacred flint. However, while Butterfly may not always be trusted because of his vanity, Caterpillar is a simple, many-footed walker through life. Like Worm, he may give advice to his "betters."

Cedar This ancient tree is used for burning and ceremonials. Its berries have been used against many contagious diseases, and the needles, made into ash and mixed with water, are used as a dye. Cedar smoke often smudges the air in Southwestern Indian ceremonies; the boughs are cut and made into ceremonial dwellings, places for chanting and healing, as well as for shade from the sun.

Corn Boy, Corn Girl, Cornmeal Carrier Corn is the most sacred of all Native American plants. Originally, it came from native grasses of Mexico and Guatemala and was brought to Turtle Island by Mexican Indians and the Carib people. Standing straight and tall, corn resembles human beings standing in rows. White corn is thought, by the Navajo, to be male; yellow corn is female. Round-headed corn symbols are men; square-headed are female. Food made from corn—especially cornmeal—is symbolic of the goodness of Mother Earth and Father Sky. Corn pollen is used in many blessing ceremonies, as is cornmeal. Strings of hardened corn kernels are made into necklaces. Corn, as Jay de Groat has put it, is "Mother Earth's workmanship."

Coyote Coyote is the inimitable trickster common to legend in most Native American tribes. Both sacred and profane, Coyote gives birth to mischief and promise, he is a deceiver, but also a deliverer of good. Through his actions, change becomes possible; and change, though good and bad, brings newness and breaks conformity.

Dawn The rising and setting of the sun are sacred times for Native Americans. The strength of the sun is believed to be at its most potent at sunrise. Therefore, players and offerings are made to the Sun Father at this time. Offerings of cornmeal follow the sun's path, going sunwise, in a circle from east, south, west, and north. Navajos describe four colors of the dawn, including afterglow. Symbolically, dawn is the beginning of the world; first light, the place the people have come from their previous worlds of darkness.

Eagle Of all birds in Native American mythology, the eagle is the most important as symbol, sacrificial/ceremonial presence, and ultimate predator/warrior. The solitary mystery and power of the eagle as perceived by the Indian was immediately grasped by the emerging nation of the United States, and "borrowed" for its logo.

Eagle People Same designation as Bear People, Snake People, Ant People.

Elder Brother First child of the union of Changing Woman and Sun Father. His earthly identity or mortal presence may also be "elder brother."

Father Sun Sun Father, Sun; not to be confused with the fiery orb of our solar system, Sun Father is a deity who carries the sun with him.

Feather As a common denominator the feather figures importantly in Native American myth, method, and tribal practice. The feather is a metaphor for flight, a messenger to the spirit world. Feathers are used decoratively, as prayer symbols, and as designs of power. Attached to an arrow, the feather becomes the universal emblem of the hunt, of flight, of finding the mark.

Fire God Deity symbol for Man's use of fire. In the Navajo creation stories, Fire God overpowers the deities who rule water. This may be seen as Man's ability to use nature in a positive way rather than be ruled by it.

First Scolder Original name for Coyote; given to him because he complained about everything.

First Woman Chief The initial woman leader of the Navajo; the beginning of maternal order, matriarchal society.

Five Horses The five horses of the Sun Father are a way of telling time, Navajo style. White shell and pearl horses represent dawn, turquoise is noon, red shell is sunset, and jet or coal is night.

Four Times The number four is representative of the four directions, the four quarters, the four seasons, and the four worlds the people passed through getting from the underworld to this one, which some tribes say is the fifth world. Thus, many things are divided into fours, and the fourth time something is done, it always comes out the best.

Four Worlds Navajo storytellers say The People came from three lower worlds before arriving in this, the fourth world. This is an important reason why the number four is of such significance to The People.

Frog Amphibian deity.

Ghost Most tribal people believe in a spiritual resonance that lives after the life cycle is over. Native American myths describe this as a Spirit rather than a ghost. Spirits that reside in certain rock formations were once living, breathing beings. There are spirits in living trees which live on in the grain of the wood, or the smoke. Though in appearance a tree is "dead," it is yet "alive." Ancestor Spirits may live in inanimate objects, confined there, as it were, from previous existence. But in human terms, the Spirit of a man usually moves—unless hindered in some way—to one of several places. The Spirit World is

often thought to be the one above this world. Yet it is also true,
in some tribes, that the Spirit World exists underneath the one
we live on now. In any case, Spirits do not come back to molest
the living unless their pattern has been broken or disturbed, or
unless they are compelled or directed to return. Many Native
American "ghost stories" describe an individual whose Spirit
leaves his body and goes to the Spirit World to join his de-
parted family members in a place that corresponds with the
Christian view of Heaven.

Grandson All Navajos are addressed by Talking God as "grandson," since he is their deitific maternal grandfather.

Great Flood Most tribes have a flood story similar to the one
in the Bible. Water, in the legends, is a primary world, a pre-
world, one that gives birth to the present one. Through the
energy of water, man is forced or driven to rise to a higher
plane. In many origin stories, The People are (as in the biblical tale) indifferent to their plight, and thus only the worthy, the "listeners," men, animals, birds, and insects, are
brought up into the next world. The flood is a purifier which
shows that the earth's creatures are somehow out of balance.
In the Creek legend, The People fish from their housetops
until they are drowned. Later, they are turned into mosqui-
toes. The Navajo version shows how Coyote stole two Water
Monster babies and brought on the flood by stealing from the
Water Monster mother. Water, in all of the stories, is a complement to Fire, a mysterious power that must be understood
in order to be used properly.

Great Snake Great Serpent, Father of all Snake People.

Great Spirit The Great Spirit has many names, including Great
Mystery, Wakanda (Siouan), and Manito (Algonquian). The
concept of a Great Spirit that is not a monotheistic deity is
difficult for some to grasp, but this is the meaning given by
Native Americans. It cannot be reduced to theology and it
encompasses many deities, forces, powers. Simply stated, it is

the energy of life, the source of it, the heartbeat of all things. Thus, this emanation of power is, or can be, felt in living and nonliving forms. The Native American belief is that all matter is animate, all things live or have that potency and potential. The life force that connects each to all and all to each is the Great Spirit.

Hand Trembler Diviner, diagnostician.

Hero Twins Same brotherly pair as Elder Brother and Younger Brother. Certain storytellers do not speak "directly" about the Hero Twins, so they may refer to them as (lower case) brothers: elder brother, younger brother. It is as if it were impolite to use the Twins' names in a story because, on earth, they have a merely mortal identity.

Holy People Given the name Yei by the Navajo, the Holy People form a pantheon of deities including Father Sun, Mother Earth, and their sons, Monster Slayer and Born of Water. The deities are creatures (Coyote), insects (Locust) as well as plants (Corn), and phenomena (Rainbow). First Man and First Woman are the spiritual essence of both corn and primal human life.

Horned Serpent A universal Amerindian concept of unification, the horned and feathered serpent is the deity from which Snake is the earthly representative. Great Snake, as he is called by many Southwestern tribes, is associated with thunder, lightning, and rain. Certain ceremonies of the Navajo are not practiced until the cold time comes, Winter, when Great Snake is asleep. Symbolically, Feathered Serpent unifies Earth and Sky, by being an amalgam of scale and feather. His power, therefore, is both earthly and heavenly.

Hozhoni The Navajo concept of oneness, of being at peace with all things in the universe, is called *hozhoni*. It means harmony within and without, above and below, all around, a circle of unbroken peacefulness of which man is merely a part.

Hummingbird Sacred bird of the Navajo and other Southwestern tribes, Hummingbird is believed to be a medicine person, the first healer of birds. The sound of Hummingbird's wings reminds The People of little bells ringing in the wind.

Indian When Christopher Columbus miscalculated his location in the West, thinking he had arrived in the East, he named the first people he saw on the Bahamian Islands of the Caribbean "Indians" (India = Indian). The rest is what we call history, or error. The first people of Turtle Island called themselves, in their myths, The People, and that is what most tribal names, once disentangled from their European/English mistranslation, mean.

Indian Bread Many different flour- or meal-derived breads are used by Native Americans. Some of these are fragile and papery, such as Zuni *piki* bread. Others, like Navajo fry bread, are flat, slightly risen pan breads. Conventional loaves baked in southwestern outdoor adobe ovens are also commonly referred to as Indian bread. The Bannock Indians of the West cooked a root-bread, which has been passed down through the generations and today is known simply as bannock.

Magpie One of the many Native American tricksters, Magpie is an audacious, clever, fun-loving, trick-playing bird. He has been known to hoodwink Coyote by appealing to Coyote's vanity. Some tribes consider the Magpie's white and blue-black feathers sacred and use them in ceremonials.

Man Primary earth dweller, Earth Man; also (plural) Earth Surface People, First Earth People, Earth People.

Medicine This is one of the most misused words in the Native American English vocabulary. In native tongue, "medicine" translated literally usually meant "mystery." A medicine man was, therefore, a mystery man. Most tribes made a distinction between a root/herb doctor and a great man of wisdom, though the two functions were frequently combined in the same person.

Messiah Around the turn of the century, Native Americans were seduced into thinking they, like the children of Israel, might be delivered from their oppressors, the Euro-American settlers. The myth of a Messiah is common in Native American mythology. The Feathered Serpent, in one incarnation, was thought to be a man with white skin and light-colored eyes. In Navajo origin tales, two white people arrived upon the plane of the fourth world, but soon vanished into the sky. The portent of this myth, like the Hopi *pahana* legend, is that one day these white brothers would return and confer knowledge of a different kind upon The People. Handsome Lake, the nineteenth-century Iroquois prophet, was a reformed alcoholic whose vision led him to preach the word of God. His was a strictly noncombative ministry, based upon peace, acceptance, and brotherhood.

Mother Earth Changing Woman, earth deity of The People.

Mountain Goddess of Hunger Also called Old Woman, she is the deity of the mountain who aids The People in finding sources of food as well as generally protecting them from harm.

Navajoland This large reservation comprises more than fifteen million acres in what is called the Four Corners of the Southwest, where Colorado, Utah, New Mexico, and Arizona meet. It is a magical, yet often desolate, landscape of mesas, plains, buttes, wind-sculpted cliffs, high mountains, and dry deserts.

Old Grandmother Ant Person A being in the primary world who combines male/female characteristics of wisdom. She is present at the time of the Place of Crossed Rivers and symbolizes the separation and joining of the sexes.

Owl The owl is a sacred, yet contradictory, bird in Native American mythology. In Kwakiutl myth, when this creature calls, it means someone is going to die. As messenger of death, the owl is not evil, but it can be foreboding. In the Pueblos along the

Rio Grande in New Mexico, the owl is definitely a bird of dark omen. In the legendary moccasin game of the Navajo, the old stories tell of how Owl tried to hide the pebble under his wing to ensure that it would always be night. He was, however, caught cheating, and that is why night and day are divided equally.

Pollen The sacred pollen of the corn plant is used by a variety of tribes in their ceremonials. As a daily tribute and sun-blessing, corn pollen is used by Navajos, Apaches, and Pueblos. The sacred grains were observed by Columbus as well as Captain John Smith. Flour blessings figure in pre-Christian and Christian mythology, and it has been suggested by some scholars that the *manna* of biblical lore is a lichen or pollen derivative. The Apaches called it *hoddentin* and gathered the sacred grains from the tule plant. Apache medicine men said that it was good for human and animal consumption, as bears sought it and ate it as readily as people. Trails of battle were blessed by pollen, as well as the trail made in the sand by the rattlesnake.

Sacred Colors, Sacred Mountains, Sacred Medicine, Sacred Earth In Native American cosmology, all things, animate and inanimate, possess life. The sacred colors may vary somewhat from tribe to tribe, but are usually an expression of the colors of the dawn, the rainbow or the setting sun (thus, blue, white, yellow, red, and black). Most tribes like the Cherokee, whose Bald Mountain figures in their mythology, have one or more sacred mountains, places on the Earth that reflect the origin or emergence stories. For the Navajo, Flint represents the armor of the Gods, the points of arrowheads; in short, Flint is very potent medicine. The Earth, as a Native American symbol, is the most sacred and the most primary. The matriarchal tribes—the Navajo, for instance—sometimes put greater faith in the Mother than the Father, and the myths show this.

Shell Shells of all kinds are used in many ways by Native Americans. The archetypal money-belt of *wampum* was once common throughout Turtle Island. The cowrie shell was considered especially sacred by Plains and other tribes, not to mention African tribes, where until the mid-1950s, it was still being used as currency.

Skinwalkers Werewolves, witches; men who dress as wolves and have supernatural powers.

Spirit World The concept of the spirit world in Native American religion and myth would seem to be almost identical to another dimension of time above or beyond this one, where the participants behave as they do here.

Stargazer Diviner, diagnostician.

Sun Dogs Guard dogs belonging to the Sun Father.

Sungazer Diviner, diagnostician.

Talking God Maternal grandfather of The People.

Trickster Creator and destroyer, affirmer and negator, the Trickster becomes a kind of animal metaphor for the plight of human beings. He is at once animal, human, hero, clown, devil, and fool who shows us the folly and force of our divine and profane ideas of life.

Turtle Amphibian deity; as the myths explain: "a clever fighter and well-protected."

Water Monster Mythological deity in the primary world who controls water, and thus The Flood that forces The People to seek an upper world.

Wind There are good and bad winds in Native American myths. Geronimo called upon Winds of Power to surround and protect his warriors. Navajo myths speak of Messenger Wind who warns the Hero Twins when they are in danger. Wind People in many of the stories are propitiated and brought into har-

mony with the Earth People, who summon them in the hope of
utilizing their power.

Younger Brother Second child of the union of Changing Woman
and Sun Father. His earthly identity or mortal presence may
also be "younger brother."

BIBLIOGRAPHY

Austin, Mary. *The Land of Little Rain*. Albuquerque: University of New Mexico Press, 1974.

Boissiere, Robert. *Po Pai Mo: The Search for White Buffalo Woman*. Santa Fe: Sunstone Press, 1983.

Capps, Benjamin. *The Indians*. New York: Time-Life Books, 1973.

Craven, Margaret. *I Heard the Owl Call My Name*. New York: Doubleday, 1973.

Curtis, Natalie. *The Indians' Book: Songs and Legends of the American Indians*. New York: Dover, 1968.

de Groat, Jay. *Whimpering Chant*. Albuquerque: Pronto Press, 1980.

Dobyns, Henry F., and Robert C. Euler. *The Navajo People*. Phoenix: Indian Tribal Series, 1972.

Edelman, Sandra A. *Summer People, Winter People: A Guide to Pueblos in the Santa Fe Area*. Santa Fe: Sunstone Press, 1974.

Hausman, Gerald. *Sitting on the Blue-Eyed Bear: Navajo Myths and Legends*. Santa Fe: Sunstone Press, 1980.

―――. *Meditations with the Navajo: Prayer-Songs and Stories of Healing and Harmony*. Santa Fe: Bear & Co., 1988.

―――. *Meditations with Animals: A Native American Bestiary*. Santa Fe: Bear & Co., 1986.

―――. *Runners*. Santa Fe: Sunstone Press, 1984.

―――. *Turtle Island Alphabet*. New York: St. Martin's Press, 1992.

Hillerman, Tony. *The Great Taos Bank Robbery and Other Indian Country Affairs*. Albuquerque: University of New Mexico Press, 1973.

Hoagland, Edward. *Walking the Dead Diamond River*. New York: Random House, 1974.

Holling, C. *The Book of Indians*. New York: Platt and Munk, 1935.

Hunt, Ben W. *Indiancraft*. Milwaukee: The Bruce Publishing Co., 1942.

Hunt, Ben W. *The Golden Book of Indian Crafts and Lore.* New York: Simon and Schuster, 1954.

Hutchens, Alma R. *Indian Herbology of North America.* Ontario: Merco, 1969.

Kloss, Phillips. *The Great Kiva: A Poetic Critique of Religion.* Santa Fe: Sunstone Press, 1980.

————. *Rainbow Obsidian.* Santa Fe: Sunstone Press, 1985.

La Farge, Oliver. *A Pictorial History of the American Indian.* New York: Crown, 1956.

Larrick, Nancy. *Room for Me and a Mountain Lion.* New York: M. Evans, 1974.

Levitas, Gloria, Frank R. Vivelo, and Jacqueline J. Vivelo. *American Indian Prose and Poetry.* New York: Capricorn, 1979.

Littlebird, Larry. *Hunter's Heart.* Santa Fe: Sunset Productions, 1991.

Lovato, Charles. *Life Under the Sun.* Santa Fe: Sunstone Press, 1982.

Metcalf, Paul. *Will West.* Asheville: Jonathan Williams, 1956.

————. *Patagoni.* Penland: The Jargon Society, 1971.

Michener, James. *Caribbean.* New York: Random House, 1989.

Mooney, James. *The Ghost Dance Religion and the Sioux Outbreak of 1890.* Chicago: The University of Chicago Press, 1965.

Newcomb, Franc Johnson, Stanley Fishler, and Mary C. Wheelwright. *A Study of Navajo Symbolism.* Cambridge: The Peabody Museum, 1956.

Rawlings, Marjorie Kinnan. *Cross Creek.* New York: Charles Scribner's Sons, 1961.

Sandner, Donald. *Navajo Symbols of Healing.* New York: Harcourt, Brace, Jovanovich, 1979.

Shephard, Paul, and Barry Sanders. *The Sacred Paw: The Bear in Nature, Myth, and Literature.* New York: Viking Penguin Inc., 1985.

Stoutenburgh, John Jr. *Dictionary of the American Indian.* New York: Philosophical Library, 1955.

Swann, Brian. *Smoothing the Ground: Essays on Native American Oral Literature.* Berkeley/Los Angeles: University of California Press, 1983.

Waters, Frank. *Masked Gods: Navajo and Pueblo Ceremonialism.* Athens: Swallow Press/Ohio University Press, 1990.